CW00346373

Moving Images, Changing Lives

Moving Images, Changing Lives

Exploring the Christian life and confirmation
with young people through film

Sarah Brush and Phil Greig

© Sarah Brush and Phil Greig 2011

Church House Publishing
Church House
Great Smith Street
London SW1P 3AZ

All rights reserved. No part of this publication may be reproduced
or stored or transmitted by any means or in any form, electronic or
mechanical, including photocopying, recording, or any information storage
and retrieval system without written permission, which should be sought
from the Copyright Administrator, Church House Publishing, Church
House, Great Smith Street, London, SW1P 3AZ.

Email: copyright@c-of-e.org.uk

The Authors have asserted their right under the Copyright, Designs
and Patents Act, 1988, to be identified as the Authors of this Work.

The opinions expressed in this book are those of the authors and
do not necessarily reflect the official policy of the General Synod or
the Archbishops' Council of the Church of England.

Scripture quotations taken mostly from the HOLY BIBLE, NEW
INTERNATIONAL VERSION, copyright © 1973, 1978, 1984 by
International Bible Society. Used by permission of Hodder & Stoughton
Ltd, a member of the Hodder Headline Ltd.

British Library Cataloguing in Publication Data

A catalogue record for this book is available from the British Library

ISBN 978 0 7151 4207 3

Printed and bound in Great Britain by CPI Anthony Rowe, Chippenham

Design by Christina Forde

Contents

Contents

Acknowledgements

We would like to thank a number of people who have helped us in putting this book together. Our special thanks go out to Murray Wilkinson, Owen Smith and Mhairi, and Chris Brown for helping us find the right scenes; to Ian for laughing so hard; to those on Facebook, at Ridley Hall and the Fort St George pub in Cambridge for helping us finalize the title, to Lucy and Michael for putting up with us through it all; to Tracey Messenger and Thomas Allain-Chapman for their encouragement and guidance on this project; and finally to the young people of Proverbs who were our guinea pigs: Vic, James, Mima, Tom, Lydia, Kate and Tom.

Introduction

This book came into being as the result of a chat on Instant Messenger between two youth workers who both use film clips regularly. We shared a vision of developing the faith of young people by relating it to something very significant in their lives. Both of us frequently use film clips with groups, and see the potential for consolidating this experience into a resource for others. Stories can be powerful things. We see the culture of films as something that engages young people and helps them reflect on deep concepts of life and meaning. We don't prize this culture above the Bible – far from it! – but we see the possibility of reaching and teaching young people through engaging with stories they understand, much as Jesus did with parables. The clips we suggest are tools to explore the gospel. It is part of our being in the world but not of the world (John 17.11–14). This is why we suggest limiting usage to two short clips in any one session. The evening should reflect more on faith than on film as the session progresses – the group may feel more comfortable discussing films at first, but should grow in confidence in you and the group to go on to discuss their faith.

The book has been trialled with groups of real-life young people preparing for Confirmation, but no book can possibly cater perfectly for every group of young people. We hope that we offer here a reasonable selection of choices for different age groups. Your group will be unique, and the needs of the young people exploring their faith will also be unique. Our suggestion of clips is purely that. If you think another film might be more suitable, then do consider using it instead. Remember – you know your group better than we do! You as leaders will bring your own experience and faith journeys to the group and you may draw on the spiritual and theological experience of those in your church, especially when discussing the big issues like salvation and the Eucharist.

Why Confirmation?

According to the Church of England, Confirmation marks the point in the Christian journey at which a person affirms for him- or herself the faith into which he or she has have been baptized and the intention to live a life of committed discipleship. This affirmation is confirmed through prayer and the laying on of hands by the confirming bishop. The Church also asks God to give the person power through the Holy Spirit to enable him or her to live in this way.

There is no right age for a person to be confirmed. Anyone who has been baptized and is old enough to answer responsibly for themselves may be confirmed. In many dioceses, however, the bishop sets a minimum age, and in this case your parish priest will be able to tell you what it is. In some dioceses children are admitted to Holy Communion when they reach an age at which they can understand the meaning of the Eucharist or Holy Communion (to the extent that any of us can understand it). This means that some young people will come to Confirmation having been participating in Holy Communion, while others will receive their first Communion after Confirmation.

The purpose of Confirmation preparation is to ensure that those who are confirmed have a proper understanding of what it means to live as a disciple of Christ within the life of the Church of England. In the Book of Common Prayer it is envisaged that this preparation will take the form of learning by heart the Apostles' Creed, the Ten Commandments, the Lord's Prayer and the Book of Common Prayer Catechism.

Today preparation focuses less on learning by rote and more on enabling young people to live a life of committed discipleship in a world of multimedia and globalized culture. We encourage young people to grow in their Christian faith through prayer, reflection, studying the Bible, participating actively in the life of the Church and demonstrating their faith in their communities.

This book aims to resource those working with young people as they prepare for Confirmation in today's world. Taking clips and language from the world of movies, and contextualizing them within contemporary Christian faith, we hope by enabling young people to synthesize their faith with their daily lives to equip a new generation of passionate and committed believers.

For further information about what the Church of England says about Confirmation, visit the 'life events' section on the Church of England website.

Young people and Confirmation

Young people mature in their faith in different ways and at different ages. It is important that they come to Confirmation with the firm personal conviction that it is right for them at that point in their lives. This means that a single church or group of churches will sometimes have a large group of young people wishing to be confirmed, and sometimes a much smaller group of one or two. This should not be a bar to preparing these young people for Confirmation. This book is designed for groups, but can be tailored for one or two. In the event of a larger number of young people, we think it is better to split into two or more groups of no more than 12. You may have young people who are not sure about being confirmed but may wish to participate in the course to explore their faith further as they think about it. Your group may also wish to continue journeying in faith together after Confirmation. Session 11 offers opportunities for exploring the possibilities. You might find the book *Get a Life* among others as a resource for this.

This course has 11 sessions (ten for before Confirmation and one following), which can run weekly or fortnightly, with the possibility of a break for socials or school holidays, so be sure to allow sufficient time before the Confirmation service itself. Young people have busy lives, so it is best to put dates on a programme in advance given to both them and their parents/carers. Inevitably some will miss a session, so be prepared to talk to them about what they missed before the next session, particularly if you had asked the group to do something in preparation for the next session. If young people miss more than one or two sessions then you may need to consider whether they are properly prepared for Confirmation.

Using this book

Although designed to be used with a group of teenagers exploring Confirmation, this book can also be used with a group as a short series not leading to Confirmation. But some sessions are tailored towards the Confirmation process so may need adapting for groups not looking towards exploring this faith commitment.

Each session has some common sections, as described below. The sessions' timings reflect the fact that most of us are only able to concentrate on something for 20 minutes at most, so we've broken up the session into sections of 5–15 minutes.

People learn in different ways. Some learn better through listening and some through visual images, while others learn through the sense of touch. To meet these different learning styles, we have endeavoured to offer a broad range of activities. Auditory and visual learners will be catered for very well through the use of the film clips, and tactile learners will benefit from the activities that involve making movie storyboards etc. The regular elements of the sessions are as follows:

Billboard

The Billboard page summarizes all you need to know for each session, including the aim of the session, an equipment list and a brief description of each element of the session and how long they should take. At the end of the page is a total running time of the session. This is obviously a guide, and timing will vary depending on your group. The equipment list gives only the things you will need for the standard session. If you are using any of the extras, please check that you have everything you need in that section.

Now showing

This tells you what the session is about, its aim and what you will need to sort out before the session.

The foyer

This is the welcome to the group. We've given you some pointers to starting the group and making people feel at home and relaxed by suggesting you offer refreshments etc.

Popcorn

An icebreaker or welcome game linked to the theme or to something to do with film – or both if we've been really inspired! This is something for everyone to get involved in, and for new groups it can be a getting-to-know-you game.

Trailers

This is when you show the first video clip introducing the session's theme.

Action

Once the group has seen the clip, this is to get them active with an introductory activity related to the theme.

Main feature

Not surprisingly, this is the meat in the sandwich (or the cheese if you're a vegetarian!). Here's the place for the main Bible study section on the week's theme, using any relevant material including video clip, music, pictures, etc.

Credits

An important part of the session is this concluding prayer and worship activity. We've tried to offer you something based around the theme for each week, but you may choose to use the same thing each week rather than changing. You could encourage the young people themselves to lead this section in turn, either preparing it in advance or using the material provided.

Review

This is a chance to summarize the learning outcomes of the session in one point.

Forthcoming attractions

We've included some follow-up tasks to set the group in preparation for the next session. Try to encourage them to see the value of doing something in between sessions which they can then bring to the group.

Extras

We know that groups of different ages will want something a little bit more appropriate to their age. Spiritual maturity varies in teenagers as it does with adults, so some teenagers will be more mature in their faith than others of a similar or older age. In order to cater for as broad a group as possible, we've suggested some alternative activities for older or younger groups of young people. When we say young, we're thinking of those aged 10–13, and when we say older we're referring to those aged 14–18. This is an approximation, not a hard and fast rule for all young people of those ages, so use your judgement and your knowledge of the young people when you choose between the various activities. If you have a mixed age group, consider using a balance of activities which appeal to as many of the group as possible. There are occasionally some additional notes in this section for those leading the group such as some background information and guidance on particular activities.

Deleted scenes

Just in case you can't get your hands on the films we've suggested or if the film itself doesn't appeal, we've also proposed some alternative clips you could use.

Screen notes

For most of the sessions there are some sheets to hand out to the members of the group. You may wish to provide a folder so group members can keep these in one place just in case you need to refer to them again later in the course.

Shortening the course

We understand that time might be an issue for people running groups. You may be preparing people for Confirmation during lunch times at school or with only a month to go to the Confirmation service. If you need to shorten the course in any way, consider covering the Main Feature, the Credits and whatever else that is appropriate you can fit into your session time. If you are not able to have all ten sessions before the Confirmation service, you could have more of the sessions after the service beginning with Session 11, which is designed to be run after the Confirmation service. Alternatively, if you don't want to have as many as 11 sessions, we consider the following to be the most important sessions:

Session 1	God in my life
Session 6	Walk the line
Session 7	The X men
Session 8	Signs
Session 11	Pay it forward

Of course, use any session that you feel you need to cover in your Confirmation course.

If you have a small group being confirmed, then we suggest you talk to other churches in your Deanery or local ecumenical partners to work together with you in exploring faith with young people.

Child protection/safeguarding guidelines

We encourage you to use best practice in working with children and young people.
We advise you to refer to your Denominational Child Protection Guidelines in working with children, young people and vulnerable adults. If you are unsure about any of these, talk to your minister or Area/Diocesan Youth Adviser.

Using videos and music in a church context
(Licences and performing rights)

If you are running the group in a private home, videos and music may be used freely, as you would at home. If, however, you are hosting the group in church premises, playing clips from a film is classed as a public showing. You should have a CVL (Church Video Licence). Check with your minister or churchwardens as they may already have this as part of a CCLI (Christian Copyright Licensing International) copyright licence. If your church does not already hold one, the licence costs between £50 and £160 depending on the size of your congregation. See (www.cvle.com) for more details. Use of material in the context of worship is deemed to be excluded from the need for a performing rights licence, whereas showing films as part of church activities in other contexts does require a performing rights licence. It is our interpretation of the law that a Confirmation class is in this sense worship, as the primary purpose of the group is the exploration of faith rather than entertainment and as such does not require a performing rights licence in addition to a church Video Licence.

As we are using clips as part of a Christian group it is worth considering our choice of films and the clips we select from them. We trust that the clips we have suggested are in sympathy with the Christian faith. We have been careful to give beginning and finishing times for clips, particularly in the case of clips that are preceded or followed by material that may not be suitable. You should preview all the clips we have suggested to ensure that they are suitable with the group that you have. If you choose to use other clips, do be careful to consider the suitability of the material to a Christian context.

Certification and clip selection

The British Board of Film Classification gives classifications to films on the basis of several factors: theme, language, nudity, sex, violence, imitable techniques, horror and drugs. These classifications refer to the legal ages for admittance to see a film in a cinema or hire a DVD or video of a film. There is no law against films being shown at home to those below the age of a classification but the BBFC discourages it except in cases where educational benefit is arguable and the age of the young person concerned is not too much younger than the classification. As a general guideline, all films classified U or PG are almost always fine to use with teenagers. Those which have been at the cinema as a 12a should be considered carefully if you have some under-12s. Films with a certificate 15 might well be all right to use with an older group but inadvisable for younger teens. If you have seen a really good film which is an 18 (for example *The Green Mile, The Passion of the Christ*, etc.) please do think very carefully and consult parents before considering using scenes. Most films classified 18 contain extreme violence, strongly sexualized scenes and a lot of bad language but they may also contain concepts which are deeply disturbing. Be wary of considering only the language/sex/violence element of a film. Remember to think about theme, horror and imitable techniques of a film. DVDs often indicate on the back if there are scenes of peril, threat or menace. We might not consider this disturbing, but to some young people the possibility of someone being hurt or killed in a film (even without any violent representation of it) might be distressing.

It is advisable to use films which are suitable to the age of your group (for example if you have under-12s a 12 certificate film might not be suitable); however, it might be possible to use particularly appropriate clips from films of a higher certification if you are sure the content is suitable and you consult parents first. In my experience, youth leaders are often more cautious of showing certificated films to young people than parents who might, for example, allow under-15s to watch films certificated 15. Remember, however, that parents may make such decisions for their own children but this does not mean youth leaders can make these decisions on their behalf. Keep in mind that showing young people a short section with no particularly inappropriate content from a film which has an age restrictive classification might send a message to young people and/or their parents that the film as a whole is 'OK to watch', so even if the scene is really good, think carefully before you use it. It is a good idea to advise parents if you are considering using a clip from a film of a higher certification, explaining your reasons for choosing it and its context in the film as a whole.

You may have noticed that some films which have been a 12a at the cinema come out as a 15 on DVD. Do check carefully as sometimes scenes have been cut for general release and restored for DVD release. For example, *Second-hand Lions* was on general release as a PG after a scene showing the use of a flick-knife was cut but this scene was restored for the DVD release with a 12 certification. Alternatively it could be that the additional content on the DVD has received a higher classification. The main feature may still be classified as it originally was. For this and any other queries about the certification of films you can consult the British Board of Film Classification website at <www.bbfc.co.uk>. The site gives not only the classification of films but also an explanation of why the classification has been given. For example, the film *Ratatouille* (August 2007) was classified as a 'U' meaning it is suitable for everyone, and the specifics of the classification were 'Contains comic violence and one use of mild language'. The site not only contains information about new films on general release and new DVD releases but also has a searchable database of all the films it has classified since 1912, with more detail for more recent films.

We've learned from experience that it is vital to watch all the clips you are thinking of using before you show them to young people. We once narrowly avoided showing a clip with an extremely strong expletive in it because we had remembered a 'really good scene' from a film but forgotten the context of the scene. Fortunately we watched the clip a couple of hours before the session and were able to find an alternative clip!

Aside from the general content of a scene, do take into consideration the personal background of the young people and their families. If one of the group has lost relatives to illness or accident, it might be very distressing to see films which represent a similar set of circumstances.

Some other things to think about when selecting clips:

- Remember to check the scenes immediately preceding and following the scene you wish to use just in case you overshoot the clip or start too early.

- Think about how much introduction you might need to give to the scene for those who have not seen the full feature.

- Consider carefully before showing a scene which gives away some vital plot points of a film, as some people might want to watch the full feature at some point.

Equipment

To use film clips with young people you don't need every piece of hi-tech gear. Of course you will need a screen that is big enough for everyone in the group to see, but a standard television should be enough. We have generally assumed that you will be using DVDs but have endeavoured to give a time as well as a DVD chapter reference so that, if you are using a video instead, you should be able to find the clip we mean.

We don't expect that everyone will own all the films we suggest, but you might well be able to borrow copies from young people in the group, other people at church or even your local library or a video/DVD rental shop or club.

Key to icons

now showing

This tells you what the session is about and what the aim of the session is and what you will need to sort out before the session.

the foyer

This is the welcome to the group. We've given you some pointers to starting the group and making people feel at home.

popcorn

An Icebreaker or welcome game linked to the theme or to something to do with film – or both if we've been really inspired!

trailers

This is when you show the first video clip introducing the session's theme.

action

Once the group has seen the clip, this is to get them active with an introductory activity related to the theme.

main feature

Unsurprisingly this is the meat in the sandwich (or the cheese if you're a vegetarian!). Main Bible study section on the week's theme.

credits

An important part of the session is this concluding prayer and worship activity. Based around the theme for each week.

review

This is a chance to summarize the learning outcomes of the session in one point.

forthcoming attractions

We've included some follow-up tasks to set the group in preparation for the next session.

extras
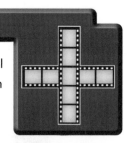
There are occasionally some additional notes for those leading the group such as some background information and guidance on particular activities.

deleted scenes

Just in case you can't get your hands on the films we've suggested or if the film itself doesn't appeal, we've also proposed some other clips.

screen notes

For most of the sessions there are some sheets to hand out to the members of the group.

a new hope: God in my life

BILLBOARD

The aim of the session is to get young people to think about the place God has in the world and in their lives

PLAN OF THE SESSION

The foyer	Setting up beforehand	
Popcorn	An icebreaker of favourite films	*(5 mins)*
Action	Explaining how the group and the sessions are going to work	*(10 mins)*
Trailers	A scene from *Bruce Almighty* and discussion	*(10 mins)*
Action	Making a storyboard of our lives	*(10 mins)*
Main feature	A discussion about God's place in the world and our lives	*(15 mins)*
Credits	Prayers using the storyboards	*(5 mins)*
Review	Recap of what we have covered	*(5 mins)*
Forthcoming attractions	Read Psalm 139 before next time	

Total running time: *60 mins*

Equipment list:
* DVD/video of *Bruce Almighty*
* DVD/video of *The Hitchhiker's Guide to the Galaxy*
* Refreshments
* Candle
* Pens
* Post-it notes
* Flipchart and pens *(or similar)*
* Equipment to play your DVDs including sound
* Storyboard handouts
* CD player, appropriate music
* Bibles

a new hope: God in my life

now showing

The aim of this session is to get young people to think about the place God has in the world and in their lives.

popcorn

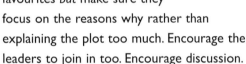

Ask people in the group to consider what their favourite film is and explain why. If people have trouble choosing, you could let them have two favourites *but* make sure they focus on the reasons why rather than explaining the plot too much. Encourage the leaders to join in too. Encourage discussion.

the foyer

Whether you're meeting in someone's home or in a space within your church or church buildings, make the room a comfortable place. The young people need to be able to see each other and the screen for the video clips. At the beginning, offer refreshments and talk to the young people, making them feel at ease. You could also have some music playing in the background. You might like to light a candle as the group starts (then blow it out at the end as a sign that the group has finished).

action

Discuss with the young people the boundaries of the group, including attending each session, openness and honesty, bringing your Bibles to each session, and confidentiality. Explain that this confirmation course is an opportunity to ask questions at any point. This group has been set up for them and the leaders want to help everyone get everything they can from attending.

Explain how the course will work. It will be made up of activities, video clips, Bible study, and there will sometimes be tasks to do at home.

Even if the group all know each other, you should explain the boundaries of the group and describe briefly what the group will be doing over the next few weeks. It would be worth asking them about their expectations and maybe explaining your expectations as leaders.

Give each member a pen and three post-it notes. Ask them to write down what their understanding of confirmation is and what their expectations are of the course. After a few minutes invite them to stick these on a wall or on a piece of flipchart and keep this. You can then refer to them throughout the course either with the group or for your own reflections as leaders. Alternatively you could give the young people loads of magazines and get them to cut out pictures and make collages expressing their feelings about confirmation.

a new hope: God in my life

trailers

Introduce this week's theme: God. As an easy entry to the course we've chosen a light-hearted clip from the film *Bruce Almighty* (you might equally pick something from the more recent *Evan Almighty*).

For those who have not seen the film, Bruce is convinced that God has conspired to make his life as difficult as possible. He has just lost his job, and in this scene we see him answering an advert for a new job.

The clip occurs at Chapter 7, 24m 27s to 29m 25s (if you want to avoid a rude word, or 24m 27s to 29m 33s if you're not too worried).

The gloves are off, God ... God is a mean kid with a magnifying glass ... Smite me, O Mighty Smiter!

Show the clip then use these questions as a discussion starter:

●   How is God portrayed in this scene?

●   What three jobs does God have? (Leader's note: janitor, caretaker and the Boss)

●   How has Bruce described God? (Leader's note: see quotation!)

●   How would *you* describe God? (Leader's note: you could use the optional sheet of names for God.)

action

In the clip we saw the filing cabinet containing the files with Bruce's life events. Ask the group:

●   What have been the important events in your lives?

Hand out the additional sheets and the plain non-coloured pencils. (Leader's note: using the coloured pencils later is significant.) Encourage the young people to use the storyboard sheets to draw or describe the important events in their lives. They may like to choose one particular event or all the key events throughout their whole lives so far. Try to get them to draw, even if they don't think

they're very good at it, but if they are reluctant, words will be OK.

Play some music in the background and offer to refill drinks.

Once the group has finished, ask for volunteers to share an important event in their life with the rest of the group.

Put the storyboards to one side for later.

Encourage the young people to take these storyboards home and keep them safe or offer to keep them all safe in an envelope until later in the course (see Session 10).

a new hope: God in my life

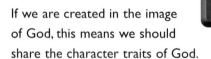
main feature

Show the clip from *The Hitchhiker's Guide to the Galaxy,* which is at 1h 36m 40s on the DVD. (Go to Chapter 24 and rewind, or Chapter 23 and fast forward.) This scene shows the reanimation of life on earth. Alternatively you could use images from nature.

In this first session, it is really good to get the young people talking, and sharing their opinions. Therefore, we have selected a rather controversial topic. You may need to keep the young people on track (rather than straying into related tangents), and the discussion might get heated. We think this is an important stage for the group to go through either now or later in the series of sessions. This is the heart of the session, so give it a good amount of time, but be sure to allow for the activities that follow.

Ask the group:

- How do you think the world was created?

- What other creation theories exist?

Read Genesis 1.21–31 and 2.19–22 – the two creation stories.

Discuss these questions:

- What do the creation stories say about people's place in the world? How should we care for our world?

- In Genesis 1, human beings are created in God's likeness; how does this make us different from the rest of creation?

- Other than from the Bible, how do we know that God exists?

- What difference does (or can) God make in a person's life?

If we are created in the image of God, this means we should share the character traits of God.

Ask the group:

- Can you see evidence of God in the life of others and yourself?

- Are there people in whom it is difficult to see God?

For other examples of God's character, read Galatians 5.22–23.

On a piece of flipchart ask the young people to list people, past and present, whom they know who have these character traits. Can they identify any of these things in each other or themselves?

Ask this question again:

- What difference does (or can) God make in a person's life?

Refer back to the storyboards. Give each young person some coloured pencils. Invite them to highlight the events in their lives where they felt God was most present with them, using the coloured pencils. (This could mean colouring in the pictures or simply highlighting, depending on artistic inclination.)

Ask the young people how they thought these events felt different from the others in their lives. Would they have felt differently if they had known that God was with them in the more difficult times?

a new hope: God in my life

credits

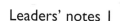

Still looking at the storyboards, encourage the young people by saying that God is with them at all times, even when they may not have felt it. Ask the group to choose their favourite colour and draw a coloured line underneath their storyboard (indicating God is with them throughout their lives, throughout time and beyond).

Invite the young people to place their storyboards in front of them on their lap as you enter into a time of prayer.

Use this prayer or something else that summarizes that we are made in God's image, that we belong to God and that God is always with us.

Lord, you are with us
in all the different parts of our lives.
You bring light to dark places
and colour when we feel life has turned grey.
We thank you for all the times you have been there.
Father, help us to feel the presence of your Spirit
with us more clearly this week.
We ask this in the name of your Son, Jesus Christ.
Amen.

review

God exists. God created the universe. We can see evidence in our own lives and the lives of others.

forthcoming attractions

Encourage the young people to read Psalm 139 as an example of God's love and creativity in the world and in our lives.

a new hope: God in my life

Main feature

You're looking at creation and God's role in it with the group. Be sure to pick up the differences between the first two chapters of Genesis – the order of creation in Genesis 1 is animals then man, but Genesis 2 has man then animals. Be aware that in Year 9 the National Curriculum has young people study evolution versus creation, so they may know a lot about this. You can have a look at the National Curriculum Unit 9B on this link: <http://tinyurl.com/ccfx9e>.

One way of explaining how we know that God exists is called the watchmaker theory – if you find a watch that is complex, you know it must have been made, not having occurred naturally.

Emphasize the importance of faith over proof, but demonstrate that there is clear evidence of God's existence in the world, such as other people's and our own experience of God in our lives, or remembering a lack of God as the 'God-shaped hole'. If you have a group which has some people who are not believers or new Christians, you could talk about that yearning that people have when they feel that something is missing but they don't know what.

With our film theme it might well be a good analogy to compare life with God as a film in colour, not black and white. You can tie this in to the activity of adding colour to their own storyboards.

You might want to bring in the story *Footprints* at this point. You should be able to find this online by searching for 'Footprints' or on a card in your local Christian bookshop. There are various versions here: <http://www.wowzone.com/fprints.htm>.

extras

For younger groups

Give each person a lump of play-dough and ask them to create something. Once they have finished, ask them to describe what they have made, how they felt making it, and how they would feel if someone disputed the fact that they had made it. Ask them how they think their creation reflects something of who they are. Now ask the questions but relate them to God.

For older groups

We suggest you have a deeper discussion debating the theories of creationism versus evolution, as these are covered by the National Curriculum, and older groups will probably have more information and more questions about creation. There is a broad spectrum of Christian belief about the creation. Some believe that the biblical accounts are entirely accurate; others consider them to be essentially true but not a factual description. There are many scientists who are Christians who believe that evolution is a plausible theory. Scientists who proposed the Big Bang theory are divided as to whether the Big Bang was caused by a higher being or was purely accidental. This discussion is not about trying to get the young people to believe a particular view of creation but to enable them to form their own opinions and perhaps equip them for discussions with those who believe that God had no part in creation and also no part in the world we live in now.

a new hope: God in my life

deleted scenes

If you can't get the DVDs we have suggested or if it doesn't suit your group, you could try the following:

The Man who sued God

The church leaders are invited to say whether or not God exists in a case where a man is suing God because the destruction of his boat was deemed as an 'Act of God'. The clip occurs at Chapter 9 1h 03m 39s to 1h 07m 02s. There are two clips which you can use from *The Hitchhiker's Guide to the Galaxy*. The first describes the earth being built, and the second shows it being brought to life.

The clips can be found at Chapter 20 1h 21m 31s to 1h 22m 26s and chapter 23 1h 36m 44s to 1h 37 m 25s.

Colour is brought to the people who are living 'pleasant lives' in Pleasantville. You can use images of the black and white world where colour is suddenly introduced along with new ideas. There are several moments where the black and white world is invaded with colour. These clips can be found at Chapter 20 0h 48m 41s to 0h 52m 13s or for a shorter clip chapter 15 0h 34m 56s or Chapter 16 0h 38m 36s onwards.

a new hope: God in my life

screen notes

The storyboard of my life

If they made a film of your life, what would be the most important events to include?
Draw pictures here or use the lines to detail them.

a new hope: God in my life

screen notes

Names for God

Advocate (1 John 2.1). Almighty (Rev. 1.8; Matt. 28.18). Alpha and Omega (Rev. 1.8; 22.13). Amen (Rev. 3.14). Apostle of our Profession (Heb. 3.1). Atoning Sacrifice for our Sins (1 John 2.2). Author of Life (Acts 3.15). Author and Perfecter of our Faith (Heb. 12.2). Author of Salvation (Heb. 2.10). Beginning and End (Rev. 22.13). Blessed and only Ruler (1 Tim. 6.15). Bread of God (John 6.33). Bread of Life (John 6.35; 6.48). Capstone (Acts 4.11; 1 Pet. 2.7). Chief Cornerstone (Eph. 2.20). Chief Shepherd (1 Pet. 5.4). Christ (1 John 2.22). Creator (John 1.3). Deliverer (Rom. 11.26). Eternal Life (1 John 1.2; 5.20). Everlasting Father (Isa. 9.6). Gate (John 10.9). Faithful and True (Rev. 19.11). Faithful Witness (Rev. 1.5). Faith and True Witness (Rev. 3.14). First and Last (Rev. 1.17; 2.8; 22.13). Firstborn from the Dead (Rev. 1.5). God (John 1.1; 20.28; Heb. 1.8; Rom. 9.5; 2 Pet. 1.1; 1 John 5.20; etc.). Good Shepherd (John 10.11,14). Great Shepherd (Heb. 13.20). Great High Priest (Heb. 4.14). Head of the Church (Eph. 1.22; 4.15; 5.23). Heir of all things (Heb. 1.2). High Priest (Heb. 2.17). Holy and True (Rev. 3.7). Holy One (Acts 3.14). Hope (1 Tim. 1.1). Hope of Glory (Col. 1.27). Horn of Salvation (Luke 1.69). I Am (John 8.58). Image of God (2 Cor. 4.4). King Eternal (1 Tim. 1.17). King of Israel (John 1.49). King of the Jews (Matt. 27.11). King of kings (1 Tim 6.15; Rev. 19.16). King of the Ages (Rev. 15.3). Lamb (Rev. 13.8). Lamb of God (John 1.29). Lamb without Blemish (1 Pet. 1.19). Last Adam (1 Cor. 15.45). Life (John 14.6; Col. 3.4). Light of the World (John 8.12). Lion of the Tribe of Judah (Rev. 5.5). Living One (Rev. 1.18). Living Stone (1 Pet. 2.4). Lord (2 Pet. 2.20). Lord of All (Acts 10.36). Lord of Glory (1 Cor. 2.8). Lord of lords (Rev. 19.16). LORD [YHWH] our Righteousness (Jer. 23.6). Man from Heaven (1 Cor. 15.48). Mediator of the New Covenant (Heb. 9.15). Mighty God (Isa. 9.6). Morning Star (Rev. 22.16). Offspring of David (Rev. 22.16). Only Begotten Son of God (John 1.18; 1 John 4.9). Our Great God and Saviour (Titus 2.13). Our Holiness (1 Cor. 1.30). Our Husband (2 Cor. 11.2). Our Protection (2 Thess. 3.3). Our Redemption (1 Cor. 1.30). Our Righteousness (1 Cor. 1.30). Our Sacrificed Passover Lamb (1 Cor. 5.7). Power of God (1 Cor. 1.24). Precious Cornerstone (1 Pet. 2.6). Prince of Peace (Isa. 9.6). Prophet (Acts 3.22). Resurrection and Life (John 11.25). Righteous Branch (Jer. 23.5). Righteous One (Acts 7.52; 1 John 2.1). Rock (1 Cor. 10.4). Root of David (Rev. 5.5; 22.16). Ruler of God's Creation (Rev. 3.14). Ruler of the Kings of the Earth (Rev. 1.5). Saviour (Eph. 5.23; Titus 1.4; 3.6; 2 Pet. 2.20). Son of David (Luke 18.39). Son of God (John 1.49; Heb. 4.14). Son of Man (Matt. 8.20). Son of the Most High God (Luke 1.32). Source of Eternal Salvation for all who obey him (Heb. 5.9). The One Mediator (1 Tim. 2.5). The Stone the builders rejected (Acts 4.11). True Bread (John 6.32). True Light (John 1.9). True Vine (John 15.1). Truth (John 1.14; 14.6). Way (John 14.6). Wisdom of God (1 Cor. 1.24). Wonderful Counsellor (Isa. 9.6). Word (John 1.1). Word of God (Rev. 19.13)

the fantastic four: the Gospels

BILLBOARD

**The aim of this session is to help young people understand
how the Gospels were written and
how we can use them to learn about Jesus**

PLAN OF THE SESSION

The foyer	Welcome and discussion of last week's Forthcoming attractions	*(5 mins)*
Popcorn	Icebreaker about session 1	*(5 mins)*
Main feature	Looking at the similarities and differences in the Gospels	*(15 mins)*
Action	Activity of putting the action of the gospel in order	*(10 mins)*
Trailers	Clip from *Big Fish* and discussion	*(10 mins)*
Credits	Writing prayers based on the letters of the word 'Gospel'	*(10 mins)*
Review	Recap of what we have covered	*(5 mins)*
Forthcoming attractions	Read one of the Gospels	*(5 mins)*

Total running time: *60 mins*

Equipment list:
* DVD/video of *Big Fish*
* Storyboard handouts
* Bibles
* Flipchart and pens
* Postcards
* Refreshments

the fantastic four: the Gospels

now showing

The aim of this session is to help young people understand how the Gospels were written and how we can use them to learn about Jesus.

popcorn

Give each of the young people a small card (you could pick up some free postcards from your local cinema with film pictures on them) and give them three minutes to write a description in 30 words of what the group did in the first session. Get the young people to share these. Highlight the differences and the similarities in the accounts.

Following on from the young people's different accounts of the last session, give a brief teaching on the accounts we have of the life of Jesus.

You should include the following:

- We have four Gospels written by four different men (with four different aims and points of view). Just like the Fantastic Four have very different powers and skills, so the Gospels reflect different characters and points of view on the life and work of Jesus.

- The Gospels were written within 100 years of Jesus' death from accounts and witnesses of those involved.

- There were many other texts, but the New Testament as we know it was generally agreed

the foyer

Once again make the room a comfortable place where the young people can see each other and the screen for the video clips. Offer refreshments and ask the young people about 'their moment of the week' – this might be something that they really enjoyed since the group was last together, something really significant, or perhaps something that was difficult. Whatever it might be, ask them to share it with the group, making them feel at ease.

Remind the young people briefly about the boundaries of the group. Ask the group how they got on with reading Psalm 139. What struck them, what did they find difficult, what did they learn about God?

main feature

by AD 397 at the latest.

- The letters of Paul and others are the earliest texts about Christians.

- The Gospel of Luke was possibly written by a companion of Paul.

- The Gospel of Mark is generally thought to be from the witness of Peter.

- The Gospel of Matthew is thought to have been written by Matthew the tax collector – though this is not certain; but his constant use of money stories is probably a good clue.

- The Gospel of John was most likely dictated by the disciple John towards the end of his life.

the fantastic four: the Gospels

action

The Gospels each give a different account of the life of Jesus. Challenge the young people to plan a film of the life of Jesus. Even if your group is less familiar with the story, this can still be an excellent activity, though you may want to prepare some cards with lots of events from the Gospel either pictorially or in word form.

Ask the group:

● What events would you include?

● What order would you put them in?

Get the young people to place the storyboard events on the floor (or on a washing-line stretched across the room) and debate what should go where, and why. Allow the young people to lead on this. If they want to put events 'out of order', get them to explain why. The exercise is about exploring what is important in the life of Jesus – not getting it right. If your group seems to want to 'get it accurate' you might want to challenge them and suggest moving the order around.

trailers

Watch a clip from the film *Big Fish*, which can be found at Chapters 26–7 1h 45m 00s to 1h 51m 15s.

This scene is the conclusion of the film in which the sceptical son gives in to the wishes of his storytelling father and tells an elaborate story about his death instead of the stark, painful reality of a painful death in an anonymous hospital ward.

After the clip, ask the group the following questions:

● Can stories which are themselves not true contain a deeper truth?

● Do you prefer a factual account or an elaborate story?

● Elaborate stories tell you a lot about the author as well as the characters – what do the Gospel accounts tell us about their writers? (*Refer to the list from the Main Feature to aid discussion.*)

You may like to write some of the group's answers on a flipchart. Remind the group that the 'stories' in the Bible are more than simply 'stories'. The stories in the Bible are not like stories in other books. They hold truth in two different ways. They are true in that they actually happened, and they also contain important *truth* about life and how God wants us to live.

the fantastic four: the Gospels

credits

Invite the young people to write a prayer based on the initials of the name of one of the Gospels or on the word 'Gospel'.

For example:

Miracle Maker   **Awesome God**
Redeemer   **King**

or

Guide us Lord
Open our hearts
Speak into our lives
Prepare us for what is to come
Embrace us in your love
Lead us into your silence.

Use these prayers together, either inviting each of the young people to say their own or, if they don't yet feel confident enough to do that, collect them in and read them. If the young people are less wordy but more artistic, you could ask them to decorate the words with pictures and use these as a focus for prayer using the examples above or your own composition.

review

We can learn about Jesus by reading the Gospels, which are each different but contain truth.

forthcoming attractions

Challenge the young people to choose one of the Gospels to read for next time. Mark is the shortest one, but Luke may be easier to read.

extras

For older groups

With an older group you could certainly give more in-depth teaching on the history of the Gospels and their outlook. A good Bible commentary (such as John Barton and John Muddiman, *The Oxford Bible Commentary*) will have a brief overview of the Gospels and their history.

We also recommend: David Wenham and Steve Walton, *Exploring the New Testament: Introducing the Gospels and Acts*, and Clive Marsh and Steve Moyise, *Jesus and the Gospels: An Introduction* (Cassell Biblical Studies).

the fantastic four: the Gospels

action

The activity we have offered for the Action section may take some time, and the young people may need some prompting.

In advance you could prepare some individual storyboard sheets (template available on Screen Notes) with pictures of various events or with simply the names of events. Have some blank ones too in case the young people want to add events you have missed.

For younger groups

For a younger group, you could make the storyboard exercise simpler by having fewer 'episodes' and giving each young person one or two of the sheets rather than expecting them to come up with them all.

deleted scenes

If you can't get the DVDs we have suggested or if it doesn't suit your group, you could try the following:

Bernard and the Genie

If you have a copy of this fantastic film, I congratulate you for great taste and ability to secure a rare gem! You can use several sections of the film where Bernard hears how his new friend was involved in some of the stories he has read in the Bible (the wedding at Cana, the feeding of the five thousand).

After watching the clip, ask your group the following questions:

● What difference does it make to hear that the Genie had been there?

● Do you learn something about the stories from this extra 'eyewitness account'?

● What would it have been like to have been there at some of the key events in the life of Jesus? Can you picture yourself there?

● How would you tell it if you had been?

For younger groups

For a less emotional scene, show a scene from *The Miracle Maker of Jesus* telling a story or of something else appropriate.

For older groups

For something more challenging on Jesus, you could use the film *Dogma*, particularly the scene on the train (which can be found at Chapter 11 1h 01m 08s to 1h 02m 00s). This scene does contain three minor swear words.

Alternatively you could use *The Life of Brian's* misrepresentation of the Sermon on the Mount (which can be found after the title credits) and discuss how some can twist the message of Jesus.

the fantastic four: the Gospels

screen notes

Storyboard of Jesus' life

Session **3**

the Fisher King: Jesus 1

BILLBOARD

The aim of the session is to learn more about Jesus' teaching

PLAN OF THE SESSION

The foyer	Discussion on last week's Forthcoming Attractions	*(10 mins)*
Popcorn	An icebreaker – movie quiz	*(10 mins)*
Trailers	A scene from *Dogma* and discussion	*(5 mins)*
Main feature	Exploring the teachings of Jesus	*(25 mins)*
Credits	The Lord's Prayer	*(5 mins)*
Review	Recap of what we have covered	*(5 mins)*
Forthcoming attractions	Read an account of the Easter story	

Total running time: *60 mins*

Equipment list:
* DVD/video of *Dogma*
* Movie quiz
  question sheet
* Pens
* Slips of paper
* Bibles
* Copies of the Lord's Prayer

the Fisher King: Jesus 1

now showing

The aim of the session is to learn more about Jesus' teaching.

popcorn

The Movie Quiz on the handout for this session is a good icebreaker which may be useful if your group don't know each other very well. Use the sheet of these questions for each member of the group. Alternatively you could put each (or some) of these questions up on large sheets and give the young people post-it notes. Get the young people to write their answers to the questions on the post-it notes and stick them on each question sheet. Be sure to keep these post-its, as you could use these films in future movie nights or sessions with the young people.

the foyer

Ask the young people how they got on trying to read one of the Gospels. Discuss which Gospels the young people read and what they thought about them. Reassure the young people that it's OK if they haven't read a whole Gospel. Encourage them to keep trying. If they have read one, suggest they try reading another. Remember to encourage rather than pressurize! Remind the group that in the last session you looked at the four Gospels and the events in Jesus' life. This week you are looking more closely at the central character.

trailers

The clip this week is from the film *Dogma*. This is a somewhat controversial film so you may wish to use an alternative clip. However, we have carefully selected this clip to be free from swearing and anything too controversial. The clip can be found exactly at Chapter 1 at 02m 17s to 03m 48s. Be sure to be precise about the start and end of this clip and if possible leave the image of the Buddy Christ on the screen during your subsequent discussion.

- Do you like the image of the Buddy Christ?
- Would this re-branding work in real life?

continued >

the Fisher King: Jesus 1

main feature

Introduce this week's theme: Jesus.

Growing in your Christian faith is about deepening your relationship with God. One way of doing that is by getting to know Jesus better. When you are getting to know a new friend, you do so by talking with them, listening to their stories and hearing what they have done and what they have to say about life. When we get to know Jesus better it's the same.

We heard last week about what Jesus did during his life. You might like to use some of the images from the storyboard exercise to remind them of this.

This week we're going to look at the stories Jesus told and the teaching he gave.

Explain to the group that Jesus taught in two different ways. At times he told people how they should live and at other times he explained life through stories called parables. The idea of these was to give people an understanding of what his message was, through things that were familiar to them. This is a lot like what we're doing in this course by using film clips.

60-second parables

Give every young person a pen and slips of paper. Put 60 seconds on the clock and ask the young people to write down on the pieces of paper as many parables of Jesus as they know. When they have written one, fold it up and throw it in the centre. When the time is up, get each of the young people to pull out some slips of paper and read the results.

Put the parables they have written into two groups – those that are in the Bible and those that were in their heads!

If they have missed a few obvious ones, add these in yourself.

Spotlight on parables

Get the young people to choose three of the parables and then get them all to find them in their Bibles. It might be useful to have a book which tells you where all the parables are in the Gospels (e.g. *Lion Handbook to the Bible*) so you can get different versions from different Gospels if you want to.

For each of the parables, get the young people (in pairs or as a whole group) to answer the following:

● Tell us the story in 30 words.

● What is the story *really* about?

● How might you rewrite this for our modern world (e.g. the Good Samaritan to the Good Hoodie)?

The teachings of Jesus

Jesus also taught in more conventional ways. Have a look at the Sermon on the Mount (Matthew 5). This is an example of a time when Jesus spoke to a large group of people about how they should live their lives and how the world should be. He talks about the Kingdom and how the world needs change in order to become like the Kingdom (Matthew 5.3–10). He tells his followers how they should work in the world (Matthew 5.13–16). He connects his teaching to that of the Old Testament (Matthew 5.17–20) and brings it afresh not just to the people of Israel but to all of humanity (Matthew 5.38–48).

continued >

the Fisher King: Jesus I

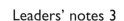

main feature

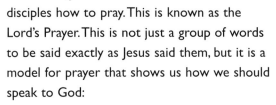

continued >

The Lord's Prayer

As part of the Sermon on the Mount, Jesus tells his disciples how to pray. This is known as the Lord's Prayer. This is not just a group of words to be said exactly as Jesus said them, but it is a model for prayer that shows us how we should speak to God:

As a familiar person (*Our Father*). We should praise God (*Hallowed be your name*) and seek his will (*Your kingdom come, your will be done*). We should also ask for things (*Give us today our daily bread*) and seek forgiveness while also forgiving others (*Forgive us our sins, as we forgive those who sin against us*). We should also ask God for guidance and protection (*Lead us not into temptation, but deliver us from evil*).

A good way to pray the Lord's Prayer is to focus on one particular line each time you say it. So you may focus today on 'Give us today our daily bread', but the next time you pray it your focus may be 'forgive us our sins'.

forthcoming attractions

Challenge the young people to read at least the account of Easter in one of the Gospels: Matthew 21—27, Mark 14—16, Luke 22—24, John 13—19.

credits

Have some copies of the Lord's Prayer available in case some peple are less confident about the words or don't know it and so that they can use it for their prayers until the next session.

Say the prayer together:

> **Our Father in heaven,**
> **hallowed be your name,**
> **your kingdom come,**
> **your will be done,**
> **on earth as in heaven.**
> **Give us today our daily bread.**
> **Forgive us our sins,**
> **as we forgive those who sin against us.**
> **Lead us not into temptation**
> **but deliver us from evil.**
> **For the kingdom, the power,**
> **and the glory are yours**
> **now and for ever.**
> **Amen.**

review

Deepening our relationship with Jesus through his teaching builds our relationship with God.

the Fisher King: Jesus 1

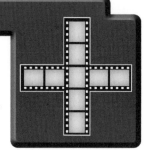

extras

Main feature

For groups with less Bible knowledge you could supply them with three parables, for example the Good Samaritan, the Lost Coin, and the Parable of the Sower. There are some good video clip resources for the Good Samaritan and the Parable of the Sower on YouTube. You can find them here:

<http://www.schoolswork.co.uk/resourcetoolkit/entry/lego-good-samaritan> (Good Samaritan); <http://www.youtube.com/watch?v=Cjuw1sPRLLs> (Sower).

You could encourage your group to make similar videos with clay or Lego or using Photostory.

deleted scenes

Watch the scene from *Toy Story* when the toys in Andy's room meet Buzz Lightyear for the first time.

You can find the scene at Chapter 6 14m 00s to 18m 50s.

After you have watched the clip together, read John 1.35–50, the calling of the first disciples.

Discuss these questions:

1   How did the toys in Andy's room react to:

    a)   a new toy being in the room?

    b)   Buzz Lightyear after they had met him?

2   What did Buzz do to convince the toys that he was genuine?

3   Why do you think the other toys believed him, and Woody did not?

4   In the reading, how did the people react to Jesus being in town?

5   Why do you think their natural response was to follow him?

6   How do you think they knew that Jesus was genuine?

the Fisher King: Jesus 1

screen notes

Movie quiz

1   What film made you laugh the hardest?

2   What film made you grab for the tissues?

3   What film made you close your eyes and grip the arms of your seat?

4. What film did you love when you were a child?

5   What film would you watch again and again?

6   What film did you love – even though you would hate to admit it?

7   What film did you really dislike?

8   What film have you fallen asleep during because you were bored?

9   What film made you happy for the rest of the day?

10   What film made you miserable?

11   What film made you think?

12   What film did you *not* see because you were too scared?

13   Name one film character you've fallen in love with.

14   Name one film character you wanted to be.

15   What was the last film you saw?

16   What's the next film you hope to see?

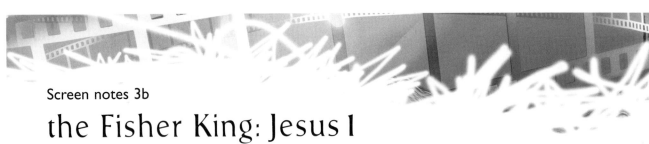

the Fisher King: Jesus 1

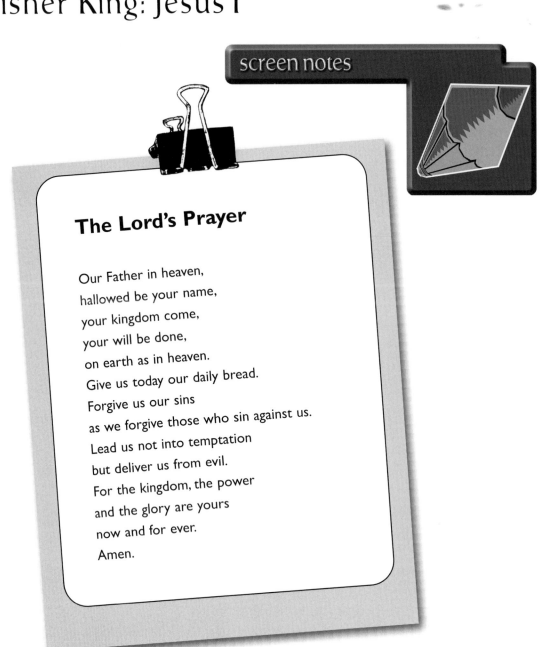

The Lord's Prayer

Our Father in heaven,
hallowed be your name,
your kingdom come,
your will be done,
on earth as in heaven.
Give us today our daily bread.
Forgive us our sins
as we forgive those who sin against us.
Lead us not into temptation
but deliver us from evil.
For the kingdom, the power
and the glory are yours
now and for ever.
Amen.

the return of the King: Jesus' death and resurrection

BILLBOARD

The aim of this session is to learn about the role of the death and resurrection of Jesus in the salvation of the world

PLAN OF THE SESSION

Popcorn	Movie Magic – needs preparation!	*(10 mins)*
Trailers	A scene from *Star Wars: A New Hope* and discussion	*(15 mins)*
Action	Dramatization or dramatic reading of the crucifixion	*(15 mins)*
Main feature	Exploring the account of the crucifixion and resurrection	*(15 mins)*
Credits	Meditation on the cross	*(10 mins)*
Review	Recap of what we have covered	*(5 mins)*
Forthcoming attractions	A sequel of the story?	

Total running time: *60 mins*

Equipment list:
* Movie Magic grids prepared in advance
* DVD/Video of *Star Wars: A New Hope*
* Jesus' words from the cross Screen Notes
* A cockerel (*a picture or a rubber chicken*)*
* Nails*
* A hammer*
* A ladder
* Coins*
* A sword
* Wine*
* A stick and sponge
* A spear
* A whip
* A cloth*
* Dice*
* A cross (*beams or a large piece of paper with a cross drawn on it*)*
* A crown of thorns*

*You may not be able to get all of these. For each of these items you could substitute the items with a picture. We consider those marked * to be the most important.*

the return of the King: Jesus' death and resurrection

now showing

The aim of this session is to learn about the role of the death and resurrection of Jesus in the salvation of the world.

the foyer

The Popcorn activity this week will take a little longer and will give people a chance to chat, so you may want to keep the opening drinks and biscuits section a little shorter this week and get stuck in to the game.

popcorn

For this week we have a game called Movie Magic. This takes some preparation in advance. Ask each member of the group to tell you in less than 20 words their favourite movie moment and the title of the film it comes from. Then type these up in a sheet like the one in the Screen Notes, and at the beginning of the session in the Popcorn section get the group going round asking each other if number X is their favourite scene. Once they have found the right person, they get that person to autograph that box. Play until someone has found everyone's favourite scene.

Recap briefly what you did last week and talk about how they had found reading the account of the Easter story.

trailers

To introduce the theme of the session, play the clip from *Star Wars: A New Hope* where Obi Wan Kenobi faces Darth Vader in combat. Chapter 38 at 1h 26m 16s to 1h 29m 10s

'If you strike me down I shall become more powerful than you can possibly imagine.'

- Does it seem right that the good guy is killed by the bad guy in this scene?

- Why do you think Obi Wan died? Do you think he sacrificed himself?

- What do you think is the difference between Darth Vader and Obi Wan Kenobi in their understanding of power?

- What is the significance of Luke Skywalker hearing Obi Wan Kenobi's voice towards the end of this clip?

- What are the parallels with the account of Jesus' death and resurrection? (*Prompt if necessary from last week's session.*)

the return of the King:
Jesus' death and resurrection

main feature

If you can, divide your group into four separate groups. Ask two groups to read the story of the crucifixion, choosing an account from a different Gospel. Ask the other two groups to read the account of the resurrection, again from two different Gospels. Our suggestions for the different versions are as follows:

- For the crucifixion: Matthew 26—27 and John 18—19.

- For the resurrection: Luke 24 and John 20—21.

After the groups have finished, come back together and discuss what they have found. Ask them:

- Were you surprised by anything that you read?

- Were you surprised by anything that was missing?

action

Prepare in advance a simple box of props as listed in the Billboard section on p. 23 to include the different elements of the story. If you are willing to put in the time, prepare the list as suggested; alternatively, prepare those with a * and suitable substitutes where possible, for example a piece of rope instead of a whip or a picture.

Having read the story directly from the Gospels, invite the groups to use the props to retell the whole story of Jesus' death and resurrection.

If the group produces a really excellent version, you might consider videoing it for use later or offering the group's performance for the whole church at Easter.

Having transferred the story from the Bible to the 'big screen', get the group to think about the importance of this 'ending' to the story of the Gospel. Often, when a book is turned into a film, they change the ending. This isn't possible with this story of course! Use this idea to discuss the importance and centrality of Jesus' death and resurrection to the Christian faith and its concept of salvation. You might want to refer to St Paul's interpretations of Jesus' death and resurrection in Romans 6.4–6. If you want a little help with discussing salvation, have a look in the Extras section.

the return of the King: Jesus' death and resurrection

credits

Make several copies of the Screen Notes with Jesus' words from the cross. Cut these out and scatter them around the room or stick them around the walls. Give the young people some time to look at them and then invite them to focus on one or two of these sets of words during the following meditation. If you have not done a meditation with the group before or if they're not used to one, you might want to explain what is going to happen. You might also want to make sure the room is more conducive to meditation by dimming the lights. If you meet in a large room, you could get the young people to spread out and lie on the floor If your room is small, make sure the young people each have their own space in which to be comfortable. If any people in the group are particularly fidgety, it might be an idea to give them something visual to focus on such as an icon, a photograph or a lighted candle as well as the words.

Meditation

Make yourself comfortable. Feel the world drop away. Let God's presence wash over you. Over your head, your shoulders, down to your arms and through to your waist, down your legs, through your knees and right to your toes.

(Pause)

Now picture yourself at the foot of a hill. There is a path winding up the hill. You look up the path and up the hill. At the top you see three crosses. You begin to walk up the path. You hear the tread of your footsteps on the path as you get nearer the top.

(Pause)

When you're at the top of the hill, you see the crosses more clearly. There are people gathered around the centre cross. You go over to join them and you can see the wood of the cross in front of you.

Looking up slightly, you can see the feet of the man upon the cross.

You see the nails that pierce them. Look up further and you see the same injuries in his hands.

Your eyes move to his head, with thorns twisted around it. He looks down at you. You see his lips moving and hear him speak to you.

(Pause)

Now you treasure those words as the sky darkens and you know that he has gone.

You begin to walk back down the hill, taking his words with you. Once again you feel the path crunch beneath your feet. You find yourself once more at the foot of the hill, looking up at the three crosses against the dark sky. The sky darkens more and more, and you realize you have your eyes closed. You are back in the room with the confirmation group and I'm inviting you, slowly, to open your eyes and come back to the present.

Would anyone like to share their experience?

the return of the King:
Jesus' death and resurrection

review

The death and resurrection of Jesus were vital to the salvation of the world.

forthcoming attractions

Between now and the next session, ask the group to think back to their dramaric version of the story. If they were filming the sequel to the story, what would they include? Ask them to write down their ideas for the next time.

extras

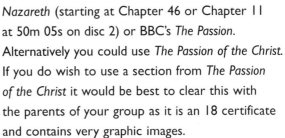

Deleted scenes
For older groups only

Although this clip contains extremely strong language, it is an excellent starter to considering Jesus' sacrifice for those aged 15 or over.

For those who haven't seen the film, *Gran Torino* is the story of Walt Kowalski, a Korean war veteran, living in a neighbourhood now dominated by an immigrant South East Asian population. He becomes embroiled in a fight with a local gang who use fear and violence to intimidate Walt's neighbours. After a particularly violent attack on his neighbour's daughter, he decides he has to do something to help his neighbours. The clip can be found at Chapter 27 1h 39m 29s to 1h 42m 08s. Leave the image of Walt 'on the cross' on the screen during your discussion:

● Walt's sacrifice led to the arrest of the violent gang members and so led to peace for Walt's neighbours. What do you think about what Walt did?

● What do you think about Walt's last words: 'Got a light? No? I got a light! . . . ?

Action

Instead of the props activity, you may choose to show the group a film portrayal of the crucifixion from *The Miracle Maker, Jesus of Nazareth* (starting at Chapter 46 or Chapter 11 at 50m 05s on disc 2) or BBC's *The Passion.* Alternatively you could use *The Passion of the Christ.* If you do wish to use a section from *The Passion of the Christ* it would be best to clear this with the parents of your group as it is an 18 certificate and contains very graphic images.

The depiction of Aslan's death on the stone table in *The Lion, the Witch and the Wardrobe* is less graphic, but, in isolation, may equally be a little disturbing for younger groups. The relevant clip can be found at Chapter 17 1h 33m 44s to 1h 40m 44s (plus Chapter 20 1h 48m 06s to 1h 50m 19s if you want the resurrection parallel). You could show only this second scene if you feel that the first one might be too disturbing.

You might also consider using a clip from *The Incredibles.* Mr Incredible is held hostage by his arch

continued >

the return of the King: Jesus' death and resurrection

continued >

nemesis who taunts him as he is raised up with his arms outstretched: Chapter 17 1h 03m 20s to 1h 09m 19s. Using this scene is a rather nuanced analogy to the crucifixion whereby the 'hero' is made powerless.

Main feature

Salvation

It is clear that the death and resurrection of Jesus were the turning points of history for Christians. All human beings are inherently sinful. No human being is completely virtuous. The Bible says, 'The wages of sin is death' (Romans 6.23).

It was because of all the sins of humanity that Jesus came as a human being and offered himself as one who was without sin. All Christians believe that Jesus' death and resurrection gave salvation. However, there are many different views about what that salvation is and how it was achieved.

Some consider:

- Jesus' death was a sacrifice which satisfied the debt humankind had to God following Adam's fall.

- The uniqueness of Christ as fully human and fully divine means that his death and subsequent resurrection rewrote the history of God's creation.

- Jesus' death put an end to death for only those who accept him into their lives,

- Jesus' death offers salvation to all people; this idea is known as universal salvation.

- The 39 Articles of Religion say, 'The Offering of Christ once made is that perfect redemption, propitiation, and satisfaction, for all the sins of the whole world, both original and actual; and there is none other satisfaction for sin, but that alone.' In other words, no matter how good we are, it is only Jesus on the cross that wipes away our sin, and the sin of everyone else in the world.

- In his death and resurrection, Jesus offers us adoption into a new life with him. We gain eternal life with God not through any virtue but by grace.

Some people associate Jesus' death with images of sacrifice in the Old Testament:

- He is often referred to as the Lamb. This is linked to the Israelites sacrificing a lamb before their 'salvation' from slavery in Egypt in Exodus 12.1–50. It was after the Passover meal, the commemoration of this 'salvation', that Jesus was arrested and crucified.

- There are also links between the story of God sacrificing his Son to save humanity and God asking Abraham to kill his son Isaac (Genesis 22.1–13).

So what makes the death of Jesus so special?

- Jesus died then came back to life, but that's not unique – he brought Lazarus back to life from death (John 11.38–44).

- Jesus' own death and resurrection was different as he was fully human and fully divine, sent by God, and his rising again was not to a normal human life but to an eternal life and glory (Philippians 2.8–11).

the return of the King:
Jesus' death and resurrection

screen notes

Jesus' words from the cross

'Father, forgive them, for they do not know what they do.'

LUKE 23.34

Jesus cried out in a loud voice, 'Father, into your hands I commend my spirit.'

LUKE 23.46

Jesus said to his mother: 'Woman, this is your son.' Then he said to the disciple: 'Ths is your mother.'

JOHN 19.26–27

'Truly, I say to you, today you will be with me in Paradise.'

LUKE 23.43

Jesus cried out in a loud voice, 'Father, into your hands I commend my spirit.'

LUKE 23.46

'My God, my God, why have you forsaken me?'

MATTHEW 27.46 AND MARK 15.34

'I thirst.'

JOHN 19.28

When Jesus had received the wine, he said, 'It is finished'; and he bowed his head and handed over the spirit.

JOHN 19.30

the return of the King: Jesus' death and resurrection

screen notes

Movie Magic grid

Scene: _____

_____

_____

_____

Name: _____

Scene: _____

_____

_____

_____

Name: _____

Scene: _____

_____

_____

_____

Name: _____

Scene: _____

_____

_____

_____

Name: _____

Scene: _____

_____

_____

_____

Name: _____

Scene: _____

_____

_____

_____

Name: _____

Write the group's favourite scenes into the boxes and leave the Name section blank for the game.

spirited away: the Holy Spirit

BILLBOARD

The aim of this session is to learn about the Holy Spirit and the fruits of the Spirit and what they can mean for us

PLAN OF THE SESSION

The foyer	Discussion on last week's Forthcoming Attractions	*(5 mins)*
Popcorn	An icebreaker based on a film of your life	*(5 mins)*
Trailers	A scene from *The Lion, the Witch and the Wardrobe* and discussion	*(5 mins)*
Action	Activity exploring the nature of the Holy Spirit	*(10–15 mins)*
Main feature	The Holy Spirit in scripture	*(20 mins)*
Credits	Prayer	*(5 mins)*
Review	Recap of what we have covered	*(5 mins)*
Forthcoming attractions	Expectations of confirmation	*(5 mins)*

Total running time: *60 mins*

Equipment list:
* DVD/video of *The Chronicles of Narnia – The Lion, the Witch and the Wardrobe*
* Bibles
* Flipchart and pens
* Wallpaper (available from most scrap stores or cheap lining paper from a DIY shop)
* Holy Spirit word cards
* Refreshments

spirited away: the Holy Spirit

now showing

The aim of this session is to learn about the Holy Spirit, the fruits of the Spirit and what they can mean for us.

the foyer

By now, the young people should be starting to relax with each other much more easily. This may mean you might want to allow a little time for informal chat over drinks and biscuits before the start. Recap briefly what you did last week and talk about how they had found the home exercise.

popcorn

In a film of your life, who would play you and why? What scenes might be most significant?

trailers

Introduce this week's theme: The Holy Spirit.

This week we are using the film *The Chronicles of Narnia – The Lion, the Witch and the Wardrobe*. Lucy watches Aslan leaving the castle at Caer Paravel and Mr Tumnus reassures her that Aslan will come back.

The clip can be found at 2h 02m 40s to 2h 03m 51s.

Lead the young people in discussion using the following questions:

- What does Mr Tumnus mean when he says, 'He's not a tame lion'?

- How is Aslan's presence guiding the children in the same way as the Holy Spirit?

- How is the Holy Spirit different?

Use these questions as a discussion starter. You may wish to write some of the group's answers on a flipchart:

- List all the words you know about the Holy Spirit.

- What does the Holy Spirit do?

spirited away: the Holy Spirit

action

Use some wallpaper and a pencil to draw around one of the members of your group by having them lie down on it.

Have the young people consider the following questions:

- The Church describes the Holy Spirit not as some vague floating thing but as one of the three persons of the Trinity. Thinking of the Holy Spirit as a person, what would he or she be like?

- What would he or she look like?

- What kind of person would he or she be?

- What kind of people would he or she hang out with?

- What would he or she do as a job?

Using the different parts of the body on the wallpaper, invite the young people to draw or write down the answers to those questions.

Encourage the young people to explore the whole subject; refer to the words the group wrote down in the Trailers section.

After you have finished, read one of the following passages:

- Luke 1.26–38.
- Matthew 28.16–20.
- John 1.29–34.
- Acts 2.1–42.

main feature

Write on a piece of flipchart the words 'The Holy Spirit' and place it in the middle of the group.

Hand out the cards with the words describing the Holy Spirit among the group, making sure they don't let anyone see which words they have.

Explain to the group that you are going to ask a person to place a word onto the piece of paper in the middle and explain in what way they think that word describes the Holy Spirit. After they have finished, open up the discussion with the rest of group by asking them, 'What do others think?' Encourage discussion and exploration of the theme. After you have discussed one word, go on to another.

Explain to the group that the Holy Spirit is a member of the Holy Trinity with Jesus the Son

and God the Father, but these three members make up one essence which is God. There can be no perfect way to understand this relationship of three in one and one in three but it can be described as like a man who is a father, son and uncle or a woman who is mother, daughter and aunt: three different personalities, roles and abilities, but in one person.

It is very difficult to describe the Holy Spirit, but the Bible is full of examples of what the Holy Spirit does. The Holy Spirit gives gifts and has power, and if the Holy Spirit lives inside of us we produce fruit (characteristics of God).

continued >

33

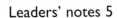

spirited away: the Holy Spirit

main feature

continued >

Read some of these passages together as a group (you don't have to use them all):

The Holy Spirit gives gifts:

Isaiah 11.2–3.

1 Corinthians 12.8–10.

Ephesians 4.11–12.

Romans 12.6–8.

The Holy Spirit has power:

The Holy Spirit is a creator – Genesis 1.1–2.

The Holy Spirit is a life giver – Genesis 2.7.

The Holy Spirit breathes life – Ezekiel 37.1–11.

The Holy Spirit lets the weak speak with boldness – Acts 2.

If the Holy Spirit lives in us we will bear fruit of the Spirit – Galatians 5.22–23.

Emphasize to the group that the Holy Spirit, as part of the Trinity, is present throughout the Bible, and is present to everyone.

credits

The Holy Spirit is not something to be afraid of, but someone to be in relationship with. If we follow Jesus, then we have the Spirit in us. We must remember to ask the Holy Spirit to fill us each day so that we may live and work in the power of the Holy Spirit.

Say this prayer together and end with the blessing from Romans 15.3:

> **Holy Spirit,**
>
> **Discerner, Comforter, Encourager,**
>
> **Living Water, Gentle Dove, Energizing force.**
>
> **As God sent you to the disciples at Pentecost,**
>
> **we ask you to come to each of us here.**
>
> **Help us discover our skills and talents**
>
> **and bring them to serve our God and our neighbours.**

Blessing

'May the God of hope fill you with all joy and peace as you trust in him, so that you may overflow with hope by the power of the Holy Spirit.'

spirited away: the Holy Spirit

review

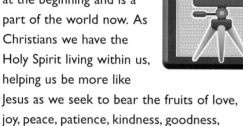

The Holy Spirit was there at the beginning and is a part of the world now. As Christians we have the Holy Spirit living within us, helping us be more like Jesus as we seek to bear the fruits of love, joy, peace, patience, kindness, goodness, faithfulness and self-control.

forthcoming attractions

For next week's session ask the young people to write down three words to describe:

- Why they want to be confirmed.

- What they are looking forward to at the confirmation service.

Main feature

For any age

Find some images or representations of the Holy Spirit from the internet. If you use Google Images, type in 'Holy Spirit'. Print some off and display around the room.

For younger children

Play a version of 'Flap the Kipper' but instead of paper fish use dove shapes. Divide the group into teams and get them into a race. They flap the newspaper to

extras

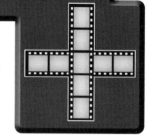

create small gusts to get the doves moving across the room. You can do a relay race by splitting each team in two, one half at each end of the room.

Alternatively you could lead the group in making origami doves.

Instructions here for doves made out of paper doilies: <http://www.origami-instructions.com/origami-dove.html> or in video form here: <http://uk.youtube.com/watch?v=-sUW0wr3jKw>.

deleted scenes

If you can't get the DVDs we have suggested or if it doesn't suit your group, you could try the following:

Star Wars: A New Hope. For those who have not seen the film, Luke is training to be a Jedi Knight, which means hard training and learning to listen to the unseen power known as 'the Force'.

Show the clip where Luke is doing a blind exercise on the Millennium Falcon, which starts at Chapter 27h 58m 10s to 1h 00m 09s.

Use these questions as a discussion starter. You

may wish to write some of the group's answers on a flipchart:

- List all the words you know about the Holy Spirit.

- How is the Force like the Holy Spirit?

- What is the difference between the Force and the Holy Spirit?

- What does the Holy Spirit do?

the return of the King: Jesus' death and resurrection

screen notes

Word cards describing the Holy Spirit

Inspiring	Indwelling	Rushing Wind
Recreating	Helper	Gift-giver
Living Fire	Comforter	Dove
Advocate	Counsellor	Breath of the Almighty
Power	Living Water	Holy Ghost

walk the line: being confirmed and living a life of faith

BILLBOARD

The aim of this session is to learn what we mean by confirmation

PLAN OF THE SESSION

The foyer	Discussion on last week's Forthcoming Attractions	*(2 mins)*
Popcorn	Testimony from a leader	*(10 mins)*
Trailers	A scene from *O Brother, Where Art Thou?* and discussion	*(10 mins)*
Action	Exploring the service of confirmation	*(15 mins)*
Main feature	What is a saint?	*(15 mins)*
Credits	The baptism promises	*(5 mins)*
Review	Recap of what we have covered	*(3 mins)*
Forthcoming attractions	How can we be modern saints?	

Total running time: *60 mins*

Equipment list:
* DVD/video of *O Brother, Where Art Thou?*
* Bibles
* Flipchart and pens
* Confirmation service sheet
* Refreshments

walk the line: being confirmed and living a life of faith

now showing

The aim of this session is to learn what we mean by confirmation.

the foyer

Over drinks, ask the young people to talk about what they are looking forward to the most at the confirmation service.

popcorn

Get one of the leaders of the group or one of the young people to share with the group how they came to faith or how their faith has grown over the years.

trailers

'**Well that's it, boys. I've been redeemed. The preacher's done washed away all my sins and transgressions. It's the straight and narrow from here on out, and heaven everlasting's my reward.**'

Introduce this week's theme: what it means to be confirmed and what living a life of faith means.

The clip for this session is from *O Brother, Where Art Thou?*

For those who have not seen the film, the three men have escaped from prison in order to get the loot from a robbery before the place it's hidden is flooded as part of a new reservoir project. In their travels they meet many different things that delay them, for good reasons and bad. In this scene they come across a group of people meeting for a baptism in the local river.

Show the clip Chapter 4 16m 20s to 18m 50s. Use these questions as a discussion starter:

- What do you think made Delmar go forward?

- How does the experience change these people?

Ask the young people to share their three words to describe:

- Why they want to be confirmed.

- What they are looking forward to at the confirmation service.

It may be a good idea to write these down and go over them after the service.

walk the line: being confirmed and living a life of faith

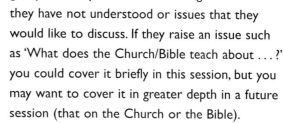

action

Being confirmed is about affirming a decision each individual makes to commit themselves to God. This means that the service of confirmation is not the beginning or the end but is an important stage of their journey. Try to get hold of the actual form of service that will be used or have a look at the *Common Worship* material either in the Services of Initiation book or online at: <http://tinyurl.com/d38s55>.

Go through the service sheet and explore and explain exactly what happens during the service. If you are unsure, then discuss this with the vicar. Alternatively, invite the vicar to come to this week's session to explain the different elements that make up the confirmation service.

What do the young people recognize from the service?

It might be particularly useful to look through the Nicene Creed or the baptism promises as a review of the beliefs we have already covered. Make this an opportunity for the group to ask questions about things they have not understood or issues that they would like to discuss. If they raise an issue such as 'What does the Church/Bible teach about . . . ?' you could cover it briefly in this session, but you may want to cover it in greater depth in a future session (that on the Church or the Bible).

If you get the opportunity to contribute to the service of confirmation, this would be a good time to get the group choosing a song, hymn or reading to include in the service.

main feature

What does a saint look like?

Get the group to split into twos or threes and draw a saint. Have them write down what kinds of things saints do and attributes they have. Share them with the group, and discuss.

Lead into the 'called to be saints' passage in Romans 1.7: 'To all in Rome who are loved by God and called to be saints: Grace and peace to you from God our Father and from the Lord Jesus Christ.'

Paul calls *all* the Christians in Rome the saints. Ask the group:

● How can you be saints?

● What saintly attributes do you see in each other?

● What can you *all* do?

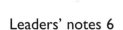

walk the line: being confirmed and living a life of faith

For the worship at the end we suggest you use something from the service sheet which the group will be using during the actual service of confirmation, such as the baptism promises, commission, confession, creed or collect.

The baptism promises

Do you reject the devil and all rebellion against God?

I reject them.

Do you renounce the deceit and corruption of evil?

I renounce them.

Do you repent of the sins that separate us from God and neighbour?

I repent of them.

Do you turn to Christ as Saviour?

I turn to Christ.

Do you submit to Christ as Lord?

I submit to Christ.

Do you come to Christ, the way, the truth and the life?

I come to Christ.

credits

The commission

Those who are baptized are called to worship and serve God.

Will you continue in the apostles' teaching and fellowship, in the breaking of bread, and in the prayers?

With the help of God, I will.

Will you persevere in resisting evil, and, whenever you fall into sin, repent and return to the Lord?

With the help of God, I will.

Will you proclaim by word and example the good news of God in Christ?

With the help of God, I will.

Will you seek and serve Christ in all people, loving your neighbour as yourself?

With the help of God, I will.

Will you acknowledge Christ's authority over human society, by prayer for the world and its leaders, by defending the weak, and by seeking peace and justice?

With the help of God, I will.

May Christ dwell in our hearts through faith, that we may be rooted and grounded in love and bring forth the fruit of the Spirit. Amen.

review

Confirmation is a personal choice, a step each of us takes individually, and a commitment to living a life of faith.

forthcoming attractions

During this week, explore ways that you can be a modern saint.

walk the line: being confirmed and living a life of faith

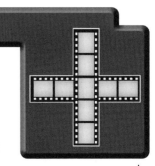

extras

For any age

With a younger group, you could get them to dress one of the group up as a saint, possibly using the Ephesians 6 passage:

Finally, be strong in the Lord and in the strength of his power. Put on the whole armour of God, so that you may be able to stand against the wiles of the devil. For our struggle is not against enemies of blood and flesh, but against the rulers, against the authorities, against the cosmic powers of this present darkness, against the spiritual forces of evil in the heavenly places. Therefore take up the whole armour of God, so that you may be able to withstand on that evil day, and having done everything, to stand firm. Stand therefore, and fasten the belt of truth around your waist, and put on the breastplate of righteousness. As shoes for your feet put on whatever will make you ready to proclaim the gospel of peace. With all of these, take the shield of faith, with which you will be able to quench all the flaming arrows of the evil one. Take the helmet of salvation, and the sword of the Spirit, which is the word of God. Pray in the Spirit at all times in every prayer and supplication. To that end keep alert and always persevere in supplication for all the saints.

For older groups

You could get them to look at the lives of some actual saints such as Cuthbert, Thomas À Becket, Catherine (of the Catherine wheel fame), Nicholas (aka Santa Claus), St Francis, David, etc. or the patron saint of your church. If in any doubt try the following website: <www.newadvent.org/cathen>.

deleted scenes

If you can't get the DVDs we have suggested or if it doesn't suit your group, you could try the following:

- *Spiderman* has a great scene with a speech from his uncle: 'With great power comes great responsibility' (Chapter 9 from 33m and 11s to 35m.

- *Evan Almighty* – focusing on everyone's choice to follow the right path or not: Chapter 6 28m 57s to 32m 16s.

the X-men: the Church

BILLBOARD

The aim of this session is to learn about the Church and how its different members are united by common beliefs as expressed in the creeds

PLAN OF THE SESSION

The foyer	Discussion on last week's Forthcoming Attractions	*(5 mins)*
Popcorn	Movie job quiz	*(5 mins)*
Trailers	A scene from *The X-Men* and discussion	*(10 mins)*
Main feature	Looking at the early Church	*(20 mins)*
Action	The modern Church	*(10–15 mins)*
Credits	The Athanasian Creed	*(5 mins)*
Review	Recap of what we have covered	*(5 mins)*
Forthcoming attractions	Looking at the Nicene Creed	

Total running time: *60 mins*

Equipment list:
* DVD/video of *The X-Men*
* Bibles
* Flipchart and pens
* Film job sheets
* Refreshments

the X-men: the Church

now showing

The aim of this session is to learn about the Church and how its different members are united by common beliefs as expressed in the creeds.

popcorn

Give each of the young people the Screen Notes with all the names on and give them five minutes to guess what each of these jobs involves.

the foyer

While you're gathering together you could chat with the young people about their church, especially if they come from different church communities. You could ask them how they first came to be members of the church community and what they most like about it.

In the last session we looked at individuals deciding to follow Christ. This week, we move to looking at Christians as a group – the Church.

In this session we will explore how the Church began and grew, and what it means to be part of the Church today.

trailers

The clip today is from *The X-Men*. For those who have not seen the film, Logan and Rogue had been attacked by a group and rescued by some strangers. Logan wakes up to find himself in an old building.

action

Reflecting on the Popcorn challenge, compare the number of jobs and tasks involved in making a film with the complex things involved in the modern Church.

'What will happen to her?' 'That's up to her. Rejoin the world as an educated young woman or stay and teach others to become what the children have affectionately called X-men.'

The clip can be found at Chapter 12 23m 03s to 27m 34s.

- How did Logan react to his new surroundings?
- What kind of welcome does he receive?
- How do you think someone entering your church for the first time would feel?

The mutants in the film are persecuted by the rest of society and find safety in the school, much like the Christians of the early Church were persecuted for their faith and many Christians around the world today are still persecuted.

the X-men: the Church

main feature

Introduce the history of the early Church using Acts 4.32–35.

All the believers were one in heart and mind. No one claimed that any of his possessions was his own, but they shared everything they had. With great power the apostles continued to testify to the resurrection of the Lord Jesus, and much grace was upon them all. There were no needy persons among them. For from time to time those who owned lands or houses sold them, brought the money from the sales and put it at the apostles' feet, and it was distributed to anyone as he had need.

- What has changed and what has stayed the same?

- What does 'Church' mean to you?

- How long has your own church existed?

- How much longer do you think it will last?

- What does the Church stand for?

- What does the Church believe?

Have a look at the Nicene Creed.

action

Get a large piece of paper and draw the outline of a church. You could be very clever and make it a large picture of your own church. Get the young people to write on it all the different things people do for the Church and that the Church does for people.

- What part do you play in your church?

- How might this change after you have been confirmed?

- What else could you do?

review

The Church is made up of lots of different members united by common beliefs as expressed in the creeds.

forthcoming attractions

During this week, reflect on the Nicene Creed – is there anything you still find difficult to understand or believe?

the X-men: the Church

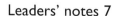

credits

Share together in an affirmation of the faith of the Church.

You could use the Nicene Creed or one of the other declarations of faith approved by the Church such as this version of the Athanasian Creed:

> **We proclaim the Church's faith in Jesus Christ.**
>
> **We believe and declare that our Lord Jesus Christ,**
>
> **the Son of God, is both divine and human.**
>
> **God, of the being of the Father,**
>
> **the only Son from before time began;**
>
> **human from the being of his mother, born in the world;**
>
> **fully God and fully human;**
>
> **human in both mind and body.**
>
> **As God he is equal to the Father,**
>
> **as human he is less than the Father.**
>
> **Although he is both divine and human,**
>
> **he is not two beings but one Christ.**
>
> **One, not by turning God into flesh,**
>
> **but by taking humanity into God;**
>
> **truly one, not by mixing humanity with Godhead,**
>
> **but by being one person.**
>
> **For as mind and body form one human being,**
>
> **so the one Christ is both divine and human.**
>
> **The Word became flesh and lived among us;**
>
> **we have seen his glory,**
>
> **the glory of the only Son from the Father,**
>
> **full of grace and truth.**

the X-men: the Church

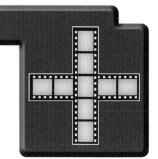
extras

Main feature

For groups of all ages you could use the sheets from Cartoon Church on 'The church of the future'. You can buy a one-off licence, or if your church already has a licence to use Dave Walker's cartoons you can use them under that licence: <http://www.cartoonchurch.com/content/cc/cartoon-worksheet-the-church-of-the-future/>.

Alternatively, try thinking about what the fundamentals of Church are. You could use Jenga blocks to build your church out of those things you think are most important by writing them on the blocks. When the young people have built the church, ask them:

● What things do you not need?

● What things are so vital that without them the Church would fall?

For older groups

You could do a brief overview of the history of the Church: <http://www.cofe.anglican.org/about/history/>; <http://justus.anglican.org/resources/timeline/>.

The Church of England gives its own summary of what it means to be an Anglican here: <http://www.cofe.anglican.org/faith/anglican/>.

For a more active session with an older group, you could suggest that they must build their church from scratch in secret:

● How would you start?

● Where would you meet?

● What would you do?

● How would you invite or welcome new members?

● How would you make decisions?

the X-men: the Church

deleted scenes

If you can't get the DVDs we have suggested or if it doesn't suit your group, you could try the following:

Dolores Umbridge's speech to the school in *Harry Potter and the Order of the Phoenix.*

The clip can be found at Chapter 9 at 30m 02s to 31m 13s.

- Dolores Umbridge runs a school according to a set of rules. Do you think she does it well? What is missing from her approach?

- Is the Church a place that should have rules?

- What rules do you think Jesus would like there to be?

For something a little less shocking you could use the boiler-room scene from *Spirited Away.* Chihiro has just arrived in the strange place which is the bath-house and needs to find her place if she wants to stay. She's been sent to the boiler room to ask for a job. The clip can be found at Chapter 3 at 21m 38s to 29m 10s.

- Chihiro even struggles with making it through the door, let alone talking to the person she meets there – can coming to a new church feel like that?

- How did it feel the first time you went to church or when you went to a new church?

- Do you feel you have found your role in the Church?

For any group: *The Lion, the Witch and the Wardrobe.* For those who have not seen the film, this scene is very early on (Chapter 2 06m 52 secs to 08m 44s). The children come to the place they will be staying as evacuees and Mrs McCready tells them *The Rules:*

> **'Professor Kirk is not accustomed to having children in his house and as such there are a few rules we need to follow. There will be no shouting ... or running. No improper use of the dumbwaiter ... NO touching of the historical artefacts! And above all, there shall be no disturbing of the Professor.'**

Show the clip. Use these questions as a discussion starter:

- How much does going to church feel like this to you?

- What rules do you have in your church?

- What rules would you have in your church?

- Does God seem like the Professor, someone who is not to be disturbed?

- What rules do you think Jesus would like there to be?

> **Love the Lord your God with all your heart and with all your soul and with all your strength and love your neighbour as yourself. (Mark 12.29–31)**

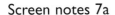

the X-men: the Church

Just the job

What do each of these film industry jobs involve?

screen notes

DOLLY GRIP   EXECUTIVE PRODUCER   BEST BOY   PROPERTIES   GRIP

FOLEY   CINEMATOGRAPHER   DIRECTOR   RIGGER   PRODUCER

1. Build, maintain and operate all the equipment that supports the camera, such as tripods, dollies, tracks, jibs, cranes and static rigs.

....

2. Co-ordinate the team of lighting technicians, and deal with all the logistics and paperwork relating to the role.

....

3. Normally defined as sounds related to movements, whether pertaining to a character or an object (footsteps, fights, fist banging on a door), or to the result of an object's movement (pouring wine, shards of glass falling from a broken window).

....

4. Install and assemble gear such as scaffolding, cables and ropes as instructed by chargehand.

....

5. Usually responsible for pushing the wheeled platform which carries the camera and the camera operator and must create smooth movements that do not distract from the onscreen action.

....

6. The driving creative force in a film's production, and acts as the crucial link between the production, technical and creative teams.

....

7. Frequently the first person to become involved in a project; they participate directly in all the main producing phases, and see the project through production, to post-production, marketing and distribution.

....

8. Supervise the work of the Producer on behalf of the studio, the financiers or the distributors, and to ensure that the film is completed on time and within budget, to agreed artistic and technical standards.

....

9. Oversee, and are responsible for, the procurement or production, inventory, care and maintenance of all objects associated with productions, ensuring that they are available on time, and within budgetary requirements.

....

10. Also known as the Director of Photography, they give a film its unique visual identity or look.

....

Answers

Dolly grip: No. 5
Executive Producer: No. 8
Best boy: No. 2
Properties: No. 9
Producer: No. 7
Cinematographer: No. 10
Grip: No. 1
Foley: No. 3
Director: No. 6
Rigger: No. 4

the return of the King: Jesus' death and resurrection

screen notes

Nicene Creed

We believe in one God, the Father, the Almighty, maker of heaven and earth, of all that is, seen and unseen. We believe in one Lord, Jesus Christ, the only Son of God, eternally begotten of the Father, God from God, Light from Light, true God from true God, begotten, not made, of one Being with the Father; through him all things were made. For us and for our salvation he came down from heaven, was incarnate of the Holy Spirit and the Virgin Mary and was made man. For our sake he was crucified under Pontius Pilate; he suffered death and was buried. On the third day he rose again in accordance with the Scriptures; he ascended into heaven and is seated at the right hand of the Father. He will come again in glory to judge the living and the dead, and his kingdom will have no end. We believe in the Holy Spirit, the Lord, the giver of life, who proceeds from the Father and the Son, who with the Father and the Son is worshipped and glorified, who has spoken through the prophets. We believe in one holy catholic and apostolic Church. We acknowledge one baptism for the forgiveness of sins. We look for the resurrection of the dead, and the life of the world to come. Amen.

Session **8**

signs: Communion/the Eucharist and the service itself

BILLBOARD

The aim of this session is to explore the central action of the Christian community in the sharing of bread and wine in memory of Jesus

PLAN OF THE SESSION

The foyer	Discussion on last week's Forthcoming Attractions over a meal	*(30 mins)*
Popcorn	What would your last meal be?	*(5 mins)*
Trailers	A scene from *Notting Hill* and discussion	*(10 mins)*
Action	Exploring the Last Supper	*(15 mins)*
Main feature	The modern Eucharist	*(15 mins)*
Credits	Sharing bread	*(10 mins)*
Review	Recap of what we have covered	*(5 mins)*
Forthcoming attractions	Thinking about our daily bread	

Total running time: *90 mins*

Equipment list:
* DVD/video of *Notting Hill*
* Bibles
* Flipchart and pens
* Communion wafers
* Refreshments

signs: Communion/the Eucharist and the service itself

now showing

The aim of this session is to explore the central action of the Christian community in the sharing of bread and wine in memory of Jesus.

the foyer

This would be a good session to have a meal together as a group. Over the meal you could discuss the fact that the 'first Communion' was over a table of a group who knew each other well and had travelled together in their journey of faith. Last week we talked about the Church, and this week we turn our attention to the central celebration of the Church – the Eucharist or Holy Communion.

popcorn

If you were told that you were going to be executed in the morning and you could have *anything* for dinner the night before, what would you have?

trailers

This week's clip comes from *Notting Hill* at Chapter 5 37m 37s to 42m 13s. For those who have not seen the film, Julia Roberts is playing a big-time movie star who has come to dinner with 'ordinary' bookshop owner Hugh Grant and his friends. They each suggest why they should get the last brownie.

> **'One day not long from now, my looks will go, they will discover I can't act and I will become some sad middle-aged woman who looks a bit like someone who was famous for a while.'**

Show the clip. Use these questions as a discussion starter:

- What did you think of the group of people?

- How did they relate to each other?

- How well did they welcome the newcomer?

- Have you shared a similar meal with people?

signs: Communion/the Eucharist and the service itself

action

Refer back to the session on the Bible when you talked about the different accounts of the Gospels and the activity you did when you all described the same session in different ways.

Get the group to find the Last Supper in the Gospels. You could tell them the following passages or ask them to look for themselves, perhaps assigning a particular Gospel to two or three people in the group. For your reference, the relevant passages are:

- Matthew 26.17–35.

- Mark 14.12–31.

- Luke 22.7–38.

- John 13—17.

The Last Supper is also mentioned by St Paul in 1 Corinthians 11.17–26, and you may wish to include that too.

Ask the group to discuss the various accounts using these questions:

- How do the accounts compare?

- What is different?

- Are you surprised to see the differences?

- Or surprised to see how similar they are?

Note the following:

- Matthew's and Mark's accounts are fairly similar – why do you think this is?

- Luke's account includes the interesting repetition of Jesus taking the cup (cup then bread then cup).

- John doesn't mention the bread and wine but focuses a lot on the gathered community which fits with what was important to John's portrayal of Jesus.

- The Passover meal is a traditional Jewish meal which Jesus shares with his friends and gives new meaning to it.

- Bread and wine feature in the Passover meal and Jesus uses these elements in a new way – a new covenant with humanity.

signs: Communion/the Eucharist and the service itself

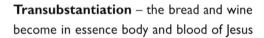
main feature

Having looked at the original events, we're now going to think about what the Church does to recall that meal. Ask the group this question:

What are the different names for the service which includes bread and wine?

When the young people have shared the names they know, explain the origin of each of those names:

- Eucharist – Thanksgiving.

- Holy Communion – coming together of the saints.

- Mass – from the Latin meaning 'sent out'.

- Last Supper.

- Lord's Table.

- Lord's Supper.

Do those different names make the service feel different?

What different ways of celebrating the Eucharist are there?

For example, silent Eucharist, a dance Eucharist, Ska Mass, Marvin Gaye Eucharist, Greenbelt picnic Eucharist, Taizé, High Mass, etc.

Share your experience of the Eucharist in different places.

Continue a discussion about the Eucharist using the questions below and responding to anything the young people come up with. Throughout the discussion let them share their views. (If your church has a particular view, share that and also share some other views of it.)

- Does it have to be bread and wine?

- What makes it a Eucharist?

- What has to happen?

- What do they think?

- What happens in the Eucharist?

Transubstantiation – the bread and wine become in essence body and blood of Jesus

or

Consubstantiation – the bread and wine are utterly changed by the consecration but remain literally bread and wine while at the same time being in essence body and blood

or

The bread and wine enable Christ to be present through the shared meal of the members of the body of Christ.

- What should happen to the bread and wine after the service?

Note

For young people who have not received Communion before, it would be good for them to try some unconsecrated bread and wine. It's sometimes best to try one this week and the other the next. So this week you could share bread or a wafer. Ask the vicar if you can have some unconsecrated wafers to familiarize the young people with what they look like, taste like, etc. If your church doesn't use wafers, use normal bread. You may like to consider seeking parents' permission regarding young people trying wine.

signs: Communion/the Eucharist and the service itself

credits

As your concluding worship, share some bread with the group. You could use the reflection below or simply have someone read the story from one of the Gospels.

The heads of wheat in the field were once individual and separate, blown by the wind, blessed by the rain, chilled by the cold and warmed by the sun, yet now are joined together in this bread. We too, though individual and separate, troubled by worries, blessed with happy times, chilled by fears and warmed with hope, like the wheat, in this bread, we come together to be God's family, joined at the table which his Son has prepared for us. As you eat your bread remember what Jesus said to his disciples: 'Do this in memory of me.' As you eat the bread, remember too how Jesus taught his disciples to act: 'Love one another, as I have loved you. By this, everyone will know that you are my disciples.' Look around the room at those who eat bread with you and pray for each of them. How may you show your love for them this week? How will you show love to all those you eat with this week? How will people know you are his disciple?

review

Central to our Christian community is sharing bread and wine together, as Jesus did with his disciples and told them to do in his memory.

forthcoming attractions

Each time you share a meal with someone this week, think of Jesus sharing that Last Supper with his disciples.

If you can't get the DVDs we have suggested, or if it doesn't suit your group, you could try the following.

deleted scenes

The Knight shares a simple meal of strawberries and milk with his fellow travellers.

For older groups

The Seventh Seal

The scene can be found at DVD Chapter 11 50m 28s to 54m 12s.

continued >

signs: Communion/the Eucharist and the service itself

deleted scenes

continued >

This is a good scene to use if your group is a little older. If they are younger they may be inclined to giggle at the Swedish or not be interested in something in black and white.

- What did you think of the scene?

- Was it like Communion even though it was not bread and wine?

For younger groups

An excellent clip for demonstrating the extraordinary and yet ordinary nature of the mystery of Holy Communion is in the animated feature *Ratatouille*. The clip is rather a spoiler for the film so it may be an idea to check if people have seen the film first. You could even have a movie night with the group to watch it. The clip can be found at Chapter 28 1h 31m 50s to 1h 34m 05s.

Use the following questions for your discussion:

- Are there any foods that bring back memories for you?

- The ratatouille brings back memories of comfort and a loving mother – how should sharing Communion make you feel?

- After they have eaten, the two men act differently. One angrily demands to know who made it, while the other wants to say 'Thank you' and waits patiently. What do you think of the different ways the two men react?

It is worth noting that the great French philosopher and writer Marcel Proust in his book *A la recherché du temps perdu (In Search of a Lost Time)* recounts how the narrator recaptures the lost memories of his childhood when he tastes biscuits he has not tasted in many years.

There is a scene in the film *Hook* when Robin Williams, playing a grown-up Peter Pan, returns to Neverland. The lost boys sit down to dinner and enjoy the meal because they see it through imaginative eyes, but Peter starves because he can't *see* any food. (The scene can be found at DVD Chapter 15 at 1h 08m and 55s to 1h 14m.) It shows that you can only join in when you look at it in the right way.

Alternatively there is the dinner scene at home with Charlie Bucket and the scene in the garden of chocolate from *Charlie and the Chocolate Factory* (either version). In the more recent version of the film starring Johnny Depp, the two contrasting scenes can be found at DVD Chapter 2 04m 03s to 5m 04s and Chapter 14 38m 47s to 42m 38s.

Credits

Instead of bread you could share Jammy Dodgers which show bread and a red heart for the wine.

If you have more time, you could use 'Table Talk' from the Iona Community Book *Jesus and Peter*. This is a dramatization of the Last Supper which involves sharing the bread and wine and reflecting on Jesus' ministry.

Session **9**

the sixth sense: prayer

BILLBOARD

The aim of the session is to learn about prayer in our lives and in the life of Jesus and to explore some new ways of praying

PLAN OF THE SESSION

The foyer	Discussion on last week's Forthcoming Attractions	*(5 mins)*
Popcorn	Special effect prayers	*(5 mins)*
Action	Why should we pray?	*(10mins)*
Trailers	A scene from *Meet the Parents* and discussion	*(5 mins)*
Main feature	Exploring ways of praying	*(25 mins)*
Credits	Using one of the ways of prayer from Main Feature to pray	*(5 mins)*
Review	Recap of what we have covered	*(5 mins)*
Forthcoming attractions	Commitment to praying daily	

Total running time: *60 mins*

Equipment list:
* DVD/video of *Meet the Parents*
* Bibles
* Flipchart and pens
* Items relevant to the prayer modes you have selected, e.g. beads, icons, rosaries, etc.
* Refreshments
* Copies of Screen Notes 9a

the sixth sense: prayer

now showing

The aim of this session is to learn about prayer in our lives and the life of Jesus and explore some new ways of praying.

popcorn

Ask the young people to think about this for a couple of minutes. If they were a film producer making a film, how would they film a scene showing someone praying and experiencing the presence of God?

the foyer

During the chat time at the start, you could explain that the session may be a little different from usual as you're focusing on and experiencing prayer. Last week we looked at the Eucharist, a central part of Christian communal life. This week we turn to prayer, which is central not only to communal life but also to the individual expression of faith. We're going to experience prayer in different ways.

action

Ask the group for ideas for why we should pray.

- The Bible has clear evidence of prayer being a way of communicating with God.

- Jesus spent a lot of time in prayer and told his disciples to do the same.

Ask group members to read one of the passages below (you don't have to read them all):

Mark 1.35: Very early in the morning, while it was still dark, Jesus got up, left the house and went off to a solitary place, where he prayed.

Luke 5.16: But Jesus often withdrew to lonely places and prayed.

Luke 6.12: One of those days Jesus went out to a mountainside to pray, and spent the night praying to God.

Luke 9.28: About eight days after Jesus said this, he took Peter, John and James with him and went up onto a mountain to pray. (See also Luke 9.18.)

John 17.1: After Jesus said this, he looked toward heaven and prayed.

Matthew 26.41: 'Keep alert and pray. Otherwise temptation will overpower you. For though the spirit is willing enough, the body is weak!'

Luke 18.1: Then Jesus told his disciples a parable to show them that they should always pray and not give up.

Matthew 7.7: 'Ask and it will be given to you; seek and you will find; knock and the door will be opened to you.'

The early Church also focused on prayer:

Acts 1.14: They all joined together constantly in prayer, along with the women and Mary the mother of Jesus, and with his brothers.

continued >

the sixth sense: prayer

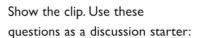

action

continued >

What does it mean to pray? Simply, it's about talking to God and listening to God. It's a conversation with God. There are many prayers in the Bible. When Jesus' disciples asked them how they should pray, he gave them these words as advice:

> 'Pray in this way:
>
> Our Father in heaven, hallowed be your name.
>
> Your kingdom come.

> Your will be done, on earth as it is in heaven.
>
> Give us this day our daily bread.
>
> And forgive us our debts, as we also have forgiven our debtors.
>
> And do not bring us to the time of trial,
>
> but rescue us from the evil one.'
>
> *(Matthew 6.9–13)*

trailers

O, dear God, thank you, you are such a good God to us. A kind and gentle and accommodating God, and we thank you, O sweet, sweet Lord of hosts for the smörgåsbord you have so aptly laid at our table this day, and each day, by day, day by day, by day, O dear Lord, three things we pray: to love thee more dearly, to see thee more clearly, to follow thee more nearly, day by day by day. Amen.

For those who have not seen the film *Meet the Parents*, Greg is meeting his fiancée's family and is asked to say Grace before the meal. Being Jewish,

he's not accustomed to Christian praying, but he has a go! The scene can be found at DVD Chapter 5 23m 57s to 25m 08s.

Show the clip. Use these questions as a discussion starter:

- Has praying sometimes felt this difficult or awkward?

- Greg uses bits of famous prayers; do you know any?

- Do you use words when you're praying?

- What different ways do you pray?

- Do you pray regularly? In the same place?

main feature

Explore some different ways of praying. We suggest you choose two or three of the following which best suit your group. Of course there are many other ways, and you may wish to select something more appropriate to your group.

continued >

the sixth sense: prayer

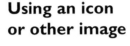

continued >

Using the five fingers on the hand

There are various models for this one, but we suggest the following:

Thumb – closest to me and 'thumbs up' for my family and friends.

Index finger – points for those in positions of leadership in the world and the Church.

Middle finger – the longest finger, representing those far away.

The ring finger – the weakest, representing those in particular need due to illness or disaster.

The little finger – the smallest and least important. This is when we pray for ourselves, only after we have prayed for all others.

Using joy cards

The word JOY is used as a focus for three areas of prayer:

> **J** – Jesus
>
> **O** – Others
>
> **Y** – Yourself

You could get the young people to make their own joy 'toblerone' using the template.

Using clay

It's a good idea to suggest some possible themes for the models such as 'our relationship with God' or 'what I'm praying for' as this gives some inspiration to those less accustomed to creative prayer of this kind. Choose music which doesn't intrude too much or direct the young people to a particular idea.

Using an icon or other image

Some people have concerns about using images of God. To pray while contemplating a picture is not to worship an idol. The image is not God but a window that helps us look towards God. The Taizé website, <www.taize.fr/en>, says this about praying with icons:

> Icons contribute to the beauty of worship. They are like windows open on the realities of the Kingdom of God, making them present in our prayer on earth. Although icons are images, they are not simply illustrations or decorations. They are symbols of the incarnation, a presence which offers to the eyes the spiritual message that the Word addresses to the ears. According to the eighth-century theologian Saint John Damascene, icons are based on the coming of Christ to earth. Our salvation is linked to the incarnation of the divine Word, and therefore to matter: 'In the past, the incorporeal and invisible God was never represented. But now that God has been manifested in the flesh and has dwelt among men, I represent the visible in God. I do not adore matter; I adore the creator of matter, who has become matter for my sake, who chose to dwell within matter and who, through matter, has caused my salvation' (*Discourse* I, 16). By the faith it expresses, by its beauty and its depth, an icon can create a space of peace and sustain an expectant waiting. It invites us to welcome salvation even in the flesh and in creation.

continued >

the sixth sense: prayer

main feature

continued >

Prayer beads

Have lots of different beads available and get the young people to select beads for particular people or events in their lives. When the group have selected their beads, they can string them together, tying a knot before and after each bead. Then play some music and invite the young people to hold the first bead and pray for what it represents, then move on to each of the beads in turn.

The rosary

This is a Roman Catholic practice by heritage, but it is also used increasingly by other Christians: <http://www.saintgabriels.org/rosary.html>.

Lectio divina

Reading the Bible and praying about the verse you're reading – this is called *lectio divina*. There are excellent guidelines for this in Mark Yaconelli's *Contemplative Youth Ministry*.

Some other quick ideas

- Using the holding cross.
- Writing a letter to God.
- Holding a stone.
- Painting to music.
- Washing hands or washing each other's hands.

review

Jesus regularly prayed, and told his disciples to do the same. There are many different ways to pray. Some ways will be more fruitful for different people.

credits

Ask the group to reflect on the experience of the various modes of prayer.

Ask the group which one of the prayer modes they would like to use together.

forthcoming attractions

Commit to praying at a certain time and in a certain place each day. If you already do this, try new models of praying.

extras

The main feature

For younger groups

This is an activity to help young people understand the importance of communicating clearly. Put one person at one end of the room with a notepad, and their partner at the other. Everyone else stands in the middle and shouts while the first person tries to get their message to their partner.

continued >

the sixth sense: prayer

extras

continued >

For older groups

Hand out the cards on the Screen Notes – how useful would they find these ways of praying?

For a younger group

You could use the dinner scene from *Signs* (cert. 12). The scene can be found at DVD Chapter 16 1h 06m 42s to 1h 09m 27s. The widowed father (a former priest who left his role after his wife was killed) refuses to pray before dinner.

- Why should we pray before meals?

- What difference does *not* praying make to this family?

Alternatively you could show the following clip from the animated feature *Ratatouille*. For those who have not seen the film, Remy the rat with high ideals about being a chef rather than eating rubbish has just been separated from his family and friends while fleeing through the sewers.

The clip can be found at Chapter 6 13m 02s to 14m 37s. Follow up the clip with these questions:

- How like your experience of prayer is Remy's conversation with Gustave?

- Sometimes it's only when we're at our lowest that we turn to God in prayer. Have you had that experience?

For any age group

Evan Almighty has a great scene when God talks to Evan's wife Joan about prayer and what happens when we pray. (Note: Joan had previously asked for the family to be closer.) The scene can be found at Chapter 13 57m 53s to 59m 37s.

deleted scenes

If you can't get the DVDs we have suggested or if it doesn't suit your group you could try the following:

- What do you think happens when we pray?

- How are prayers answered?

For older groups

Talladega Nights: The Ballad of Ricky Bobby includes an interesting (perhaps dubious!) discussion about the nature of prayer surrounding Ricky Bobby's choice of words for Grace before a meal:

> **Dear Lord Baby Jesus . . ., we thank you so much for this bountiful harvest, . . . I just wanna take time to say thank you for my family, my two beautiful beautiful handsome and striking sons, Walker and Texas Ranger . . . and of course my Red-Hot Smokin' Wife, Carley.**

The scene can be found at Chapter 4 12m 00s to 15m 00s. Warning: there is one mild expletive in the scene and there are more expletives following this scene, so be careful about where you end the clip (we suggest with the words 'I'm not gonna lie to you, it felt good'.)

- Ricky Bobby prefers to pray to baby Jesus – what do you think about this?

- Do you think of yourself as praying to a particular aspect of God?

- Is it right for Ricky Bobby to pray like this?

the sixth sense: prayer

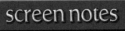

screen notes

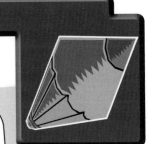

Prayer promises

I commit to pray:

At   o'clock.

In my room/the garden/school/bus shelter.

About:

My friends/my family/the Church/the world/saying sorry.

And by

Listening.

the sixth sense: prayer

Toblerone sheet

✂

Jesus	**Others**	**Yourself**	Stick with glue here

the sixth sense: prayer

screen notes

Some ideas for prayer

Lots of people find that they connect to God not only by traditional quiet, eyes-shut prayer but also in other ways. We're not saying that these will all work for you, but give them a try as a starting point.

GO FOR A WALK	LAUGH	CRY
SWIM	SIT ON A CUSHION	LOOK AT THE STARS
HELP SOMEONE	IMAGINE YOU'RE PHONING GOD	MESS AROUND WITH SOME PAINT/PENS
FAST	LOOK AT A SUNSET	WRITE A LETTER TO GOD
MAKE A FRIENDSHIP BRACELET	DO SOMETHING NEW	GO SAILING
CLIMB A TREE	SIT IN A FIELD	GO FOR A CYCLE RIDE
LOOK AT CLOUDS	THINK ABOUT SOMEONE DIFFERENT EVERY DAY	HUG A TREE
LISTEN TO THE RAIN	READ A BIBLE STUDY	PLAY AN INSTRUMENT
CUDDLE A TEDDY BEAR	WATCH A STORM	WORK IN THE GARDEN
FLY IN A PLANE	LOOK AT A RAINBOW	LOOK AT A SUNRISE
KEEP A PRAYER DIARY	CLIMB A MOUNTAIN	IMAGINE YOU'RE TEXTING GOD
PRAY FOR EACH OF YOUR FRIENDS IN TURN	LOOK AT SOME FAMILY PHOTOS AND PRAY FOR THEM	PRAY FOR PEOPLE ON YOUR SOCIAL NETWORKS
DOWNLOAD A REGULAR PRAYER PODCAST	VISIT AN OLD CHURCH	ADD A BIBLE/PRAYER APPLICATION TO YOUR FACEBOOK PAGE

lost in translation: the Bible

BILLBOARD

The aim of this session is to learn more about the Bible and its various books

PLAN OF THE SESSION

The foyer	Discussion on last week's Forthcoming Attractions	*(5 mins)*
Popcorn	Bible race	*(5 mins)*
Trailers	A scene from *The Day After Tomorrow* and discussion	*(5 mins)*
Action	DVD sort	*(10 mins)*
Main feature	Getting to know the Bible	*(20 mins)*
Credits	Favourite Bible verses	*(10 mins)*
Review	Recap of what we have covered	*(5 mins)*
Forthcoming attractions	Daily Bible reading notes	

Total running time: *60 mins*

Equipment list:
* DVD/video of *The Day After Tomorrow*
* Bibles
* Flipchart and pens
* DVDs of different kinds
* Refreshments
* Images of Bible texts in Greek and Hebrew
* Screen notes

lost in translation: the Bible

now showing

The aim of this session is to learn more about the Bible and its various books.

popcorn

For the opening game this week, get the group to take out their Bibles and see who can be the fastest to find certain passages. For example, you could use: first person to find – shortest psalm, longest psalm, Noah, Elijah on the mount of Carmel, Jonah in the whale, Daniel in the lion's den, Jesus being tempted, the seven letters to the churches, the last word in the whole Bible, etc. For alternative opening activities with little or no Bible knowledge or for those who know their Bibles very well, see Extras.

the foyer

Talking about our prayer lives can be very difficult for Christians as we often feel guilty that we don't pray long enough or hard enough. Keep this in mind as you ask the group about their experiences of prayer since you last met. In the last two sessions we have covered the Eucharist and prayer; this week we turn to another fundamental practice of Christians, reading the Bible

trailers

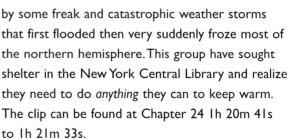

Introduce this week's theme: the Bible.

The Day After Tomorrow

For those who have not seen the film, the world has been struck by some freak and catastrophic weather storms that first flooded then very suddenly froze most of the northern hemisphere. This group have sought shelter in the New York Central Library and realize they need to do *anything* they can to keep warm. The clip can be found at Chapter 24 1h 20m 41s to 1h 21m 33s.

Show the clip. Use these questions as a discussion starter:

- Why was it so important to preserve the Gutenberg Bible?

- What other book would you save, and why?

lost in translation: the Bible

action

Split the young people into groups of about four or five and give each group a stack of DVDs and videos. Make sure there is a variety of subjects (including instructional exercise, sports, documentaries, music, biographies, histories, etc. from both TV and film) and with various certifications. Ask the young people to 'put them in order' and give no further clarification or suggestion. Give the groups a few minutes and when they seem to have an 'order', ask each group how they ordered them. You can repeat this again, asking them to put them in a different order. If you think your group are struggling you could suggest different 'orders': alphabetical, certification, date made, type of film, length of film, period they're about, etc.

main feature

Following on from this activity, go on to talk to the young people about the different types of books in the Bible (you might want to do this with the Bible Library activity in the Extras). Explain that the books of the Bible can be grouped as different types of books as on the screen notes.

Law/history

At the beginning of the Bible there are five books which as a group are called just that in Greek – 'the five books' or Pentateuch (meaning five books). The Jewish people call them the Torah or books of law. These books tell the early history of God's people (the people of Israel) including Moses receiving the laws for the people of Israel. Other books, such as Kings, tell the later history of the Jewish people. The Acts of the Apostles is a similar book about the early history of the Christian people or followers of the way.

Poetry/wisdom

Another five books in the Old Testament also fall in a group. They have a lot of word pictures or imagery. Some call these books poetic or wisdom literature. For example, you may know some of the Psalms. Some of them are now sung as hymns and worship songs.

Prophecy

Many of the books of the Old Testament contain visions which God sent to some people we call prophets. Not every word in these books is prophecy, some are about the lives of those prophets, like the story of Jonah. Some of the prophecies are also in very symbolic language so can take a little time to understand. Sometimes people also divide this group of books into the Major Prophets (the longer books) and the Minor Prophets (the shorter books towards the end of the Old Testament). The New Testament also finishes with a book of prophecy about the end of the world.

Gospels

The word 'gospel' means 'Good News'. The New Testament has four accounts of the Good News story of Jesus – those called Matthew, Mark, Luke and John. They are four different views of the life of Jesus. They have a lot in common and some contain bits which others don't. The author of the Gospel of Luke also wrote the Acts of the Apostles.

continued >

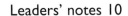

lost in translation: the Bible

continued >

Letters

Most of the New Testament is actually a collection of letters. Many of these were written by a man called Paul who never met Jesus during his lifetime but who saw him in a vision after Jesus had died and risen. Paul then travelled around to different cities preaching the Good News, then kept in touch via letter with the people he had preached to when he was elsewhere. They are a good source for people who have just started in faith as they are often written to people who have just heard about Jesus. There are also letters from Paul to individuals and letters from some of the disciples who are described in the Gospels and Acts.

You have now explored the books that make up the Bible: time for some more detail . . .

If your group is really not familiar with the Bible, it may also be an idea to cover the whole concept of chapters and verses – which were not in the original texts (nor were full stops or commas!), but are used now so that we all know which bit we mean.

Explain that when we mention a Bible passage, we say which book it comes from, what chapter and which verses, such as Luke 14 verse 34. There are a few books that don't have chapters, so we just say the name of the book and then the verses, such as Jude 3–4.

main feature

Now, if your knowledge of the Bible is expansive, feel free to talk about it as you feel best. If you feel you need a little help, look in the Extras.

Whatever your Bible knowledge, you won't manage to cover everything in this session, so try to focus on some key points you want the young people to remember which will help them when they're reading their Bible in the future.

Find some images of the original languages of the Bible (Hebrew and Greek) on the internet and show these to the young people.

Follow the explanation of the Bible with this activity:

Hand out the cards of various events in the Bible and get the young people to put them into order. You can follow this activity with talking about the different chronologies of the Bible – when the events happened and when the books of the Bible were written.

Discussion

Get the group to think about the basics of the formation of the Bible as a collection of books just like the DVDs they sorted. Emphasize what different types of books there are.

credits

Produce several cards with passages of the Bible and scatter them around the room. Ask the group to choose one or two of the passages and, if they feel comfortable, explain why. For some suggested passages, see the Screen Notes, but do be sure to add any passages which you think are more appropriate to your group.

For the prayer this week, invite them to read in turn the passage that means most to them, even if it's repeated. You could put some music on in the background while the young people read their passages, and then conclude with your own chosen passage.

lost in translation: the Bible

review

The Bible is a rich library of many different types of writing which we should read regularly as part of our Christian practice.

extras

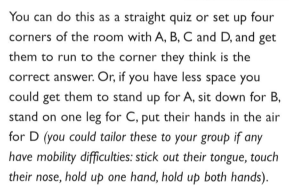

Popcorn

For groups with little or no knowledge of the Bible

See multiple-choice quiz sheet.

You can do this as a straight quiz or set up four corners of the room with A, B, C and D, and get them to run to the corner they think is the correct answer. Or, if you have less space you could get them to stand up for A, sit down for B, stand on one leg for C, put their hands in the air for D (you could tailor these to your group if any have mobility difficulties: stick out their tongue, touch their nose, hold up one hand, hold up both hands).

For those with a deeper knowledge of the Bible

As above, but with greater levels of difficulty:

- Esther becomes queen.
- David slays Goliath.
- God speaks to Job.
- The coming of the Holy Spirit.
- Moses is given the tablets with the Ten Commandments on.
- Nehemiah rebuilds the walls of Jerusalem.
- A psalm which begins 'Out of the depths I cry to you'.
- At the name of Jesus, every knee shall bow.
- Pilate washes his hands.
- Who does Luke write Acts for?

forthcoming attractions

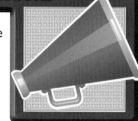

Find or suggest some daily Bible reading notes for young people either in the form of monthly/ yearly subscriptions to magazines or via daily email/podcast: WordLive: <http://www.scriptureunion.org.uk/wordlive>; SUbmerge: <http://www.scriptureunion.org.uk/ SUbmerge/1015.id>.

Various options from CWR: <http://www.cwrstore.org.uk/ Merchant2/merchant.mvc?screen=SUBSCRIPTIONS> .BRF: <http://www.biblereadingnotes.org.uk/>.

This is the last session before the confirmation. Be sure to discuss the times of rehearsal (if there is one) and the actual service.

Action

The Bible library

Have strips of paper each with a name of a book of the Bible on. Get the young people to sort them into Old and New Testaments. Then move them into Gospels, laws, letters, prophets, histories. You could provide each of the young people with their own set and make a 'bookcase' of the Bible, getting them to colour-code them according to type.

There are various choices with this activity. You can give the young people the books already colour-coded or not, you can include the books of the Apocrypha or not. It depends how much time you think you have. You can also do one big bookcase together as a group, maybe giving different members of the group a few books each or get the young people to do it individually.

continued >

lost in translation: the Bible

extras

continued >

Main feature

For older groups

There is a great exercise from the Bible Society you can do. Put the young people into small groups and give them a handful of bits of paper with names of the books of the Bible on them. By trading they must seek to build the best Bible they can. (*You'll need two complete sets of the books of the Bible plus an extra of each Psalms, Mark, Acts and Romans.*) You can hold some back and produce them as 'recent discoveries' after a few minutes. After the exercise, get young people to talk about their Bibles – what did they *definitely* want? What meant their Bible was sufficiently complete? What about the other books?

Bible teaching notes

The Bible was first translated into Latin as early as the year 300, much of it by St Jerome.

The Bible was first translated into English in the 1380s by John Wycliffe (the Wycliffe Bible translators continue his work today in translating the Bible into every language in the world).

This was just in his handwriting, though, as printing presses weren't invented until the late medieval period by a man named Gutenberg. The first thing he printed was a Latin Bible (as shown in the clip from *The Day After Tomorrow*). The first New Testaments in English were printed in 1525 by William Tyndale, and the whole Bible was printed in English in 1535 (this was when Henry VIII was king).

The Bible didn't just appear one day but was written

about a long period of time *over* a long period of time.

Academics can't even agree when all the books were written or who wrote all of them.

Since then there have been many different English translations of the Bible, and some non-verbal versions too like *The Graphic Bible, The Manga Bible* and films. The Bible is now translated into many different languages so we and millions of other people can read it in our own language.

Take a look at the same passage in various different translations. For example, find John 1.1 in various versions.

However, today about 200 million people do not have the Bible in their own language.

Bible timeline

Get the young people to think about the context in which the different books were written by using the timelines (e.g. books written during the Babylonian exile such as Lamentations or books written after Jesus' death and resurrection).

You might find it useful to use the Bible storyboard cards to create a basic timeline of the stories in the Bible.

You might want to explore the timeline and how the books of the Bible fit in.

The Bible Society describes the Bible story as a whole like this:

continued >

lost in translation: the Bible

extras

continued >

Act 1: God establishes his kingdom – creation.

Act 2: Rebellion in the kingdom – fall.

Act 3: The King chooses Israel – redemption initiated.

Scene 1: A people for the King.

Scene 2: A land for his people.

Interlude: A kingdom story waiting for an ending – the intertestamental period.

Act 4: The coming of the King – redemption accomplished.

Act 5: Spreading the news of the King – the mission of the Church.

Scene 1: From Jerusalem to Rome.

Scene 2: And into all the world.

Act 6: The return of the King – redemption completed.

deleted scenes

If you can't get the DVDs we have suggested or if it doesn't suit your group, you could try the following: if you didn't use it last week, you can use the clip from *Ratatouille*. Remy the rat with high ideals about being a chef rather than eating rubbish has just been separated from his family and friends while fleeing through the sewers. He looks for something to guide him in the book of the great chef whom he so admires.

The clip can be found at Chapter 6 13m 02s to 14m 37s.

Follow up the clip with these questions:

- Do you sometimes wish the Bible would speak to you when you read it?

- Would it help if the instructions were as direct?

- How do you read the Bible? In whole chapters at a time? Verse by verse?

lost in translation: the Bible

screen notes

Multiple-choice quiz

To help you when running it, the correct answers are **in bold**.

1 How many books are there in the Bible?

  a 6

  b **66**

  c 600

  d 6,000

2 Who wrote the Bible?

  a God

  b Jesus

  c **Lots of different people over the years**

  d The Archbishop of Canterbury

3 The Bible is divided into two Testaments. What are they called?

  a George and Harry

  b The First Testament and the Second Testament

  c Genesis and Exodus

  d **The Old Testament and the New Testament**

4 What story is at the very beginning of the Bible?

  a **Creation**

  b The life of Jesus

  c Noah and the Ark

  d The Good Samaritan

5 Which Testament features the life of Jesus?

  a Both the Old and the New

  b Mostly the Old but a bit in the New

  c Just the Old Testament

  d **Just the New Testament**

6 Which one of these characters does not feature in the Bible?

  a Noah

  b Jonah

  c **Ned Flanders**

  d Mary Magdalene

7 Someone wrote lots of letters which are in the New Testament, his name was:

  a John

  b **Paul**

  c George

  d Ringo

8 There are four Gospels in the New Testament, which are they?

  a **Mark, Matthew, Luke and John**

  b Paul, John, Peter, Andrew

  c Mary, Thomas, Peter and Jude

  d Joanna, Thaddeus, Judas and John

lost in translation: the Bible

screen notes

Events in the Bible

1   John had a vision of heaven on the Isle of Patmos.

2. Joseph was sold into slavery by his jealous brothers and was then sent to Egypt.

3   Jesus was raised from the dead.

4   Moses crossed the Red Sea with the Hebrews running away from Pharaoh.

5   Daniel was thrown into the den of lions.

6   Samson fell in love with Delilah and told her his secret.

7   Jonah was swallowed by a giant fish.

8   Noah built an ark in obedience to God.

9   Mary was visited by the angel Gabriel who told her she was going to have a child – the Son of God.

10 Naomi sends Ruth to glean the fields of Boaz.

Answers:

1	Revelation.	6	Judges 16.
2	Genesis 37.12.	7	Jonah 1.17.
3	Luke 24.1–12.	8	Genesis 6.
4	Exodus 14.21–31.	9	Luke 1.26–38.
5	Daniel 6.	10	Ruth.

lost in translation: the Bible

Passages from the Bible

screen notes

But as for you, man of God, shun all this; pursue righteousness, godliness, faith, love, endurance, gentleness. Fight the good fight of the faith; take hold of the eternal life to which you were recalled and for which you made the good confession in the presence of many witnesses. (*1 Timothy 6.11–12*)

There are different kinds of service, but the same Lord. There are different kinds of working, but the same God works all of them in all people. (*1 Corinthians 12.5–7*)

Even though I walk through the valley of the shadow of death, I will fear no evil, for you are with me; your rod and your staff, they comfort me. (*Psalm 23.4*)

The thief comes only to steal and kill and destroy; I have come that they may have life, and have it to the full. (*John 10.10*)

The man who plants and the man who waters have one purpose, and each will be rewarded according to his own labour. For we are God's fellow workers; you are God's field, God's building. (*1 Corinthians 3.8–9*)

But the fruit of the Spirit is love, joy, peace, patience, kindness, goodness, faithfulness, gentleness and self-control. Against such things there is no law. (*Galatians 5.22–23*)

Finally, brothers and sisters, whatever is true, whatever is noble, whatever is right, whatever is pure, whatever is lovely, whatever is admirable – if anything is excellent or praiseworthy – think about such things. Whatever you have learned or received or heard from me, or seen in me – put it into practice. And the God of peace will be with you. (*Philippians 4.8–9*)

For I know the plans I have for you. Plans for good and not for evil to give you a future and a hope. (*Jeremiah 29.11*)

The Word became flesh and blood, and moved into the neighbourhood. We saw the glory with our own eyes, the one-of-a-kind glory, like Father, like Son, Generous inside and out, true from start to finish. (*John 1.14, The Message*)

If I have the gift of prophecy and can fathom all mysteries and all knowledge, and if I have a faith that can move mountains, but have not love, I am nothing. If I give all I possess to the poor and surrender my body to the flames, but have not love, I gain nothing. (*1 Corinthians 13.2–4*)

Here I am! I stand at the door and knock. If anyone hears my voice and opens the door, I will come in and eat with him, and he with me. (*Revelation 3.20*)

Peace I leave with you; my peace I give you. I do not give to you as the world gives. Do not let your hearts be troubled and do not be afraid. (*John 14.27*)

There is a time for everything, and a season for every activity under heaven. (*Ecclesiastes 3.1*)

Look at the birds of the air; they do not sow or reap or store away in barns, and yet your heavenly Father feeds them. Are you not much more valuable than they? Who of you by worrying can add a single hour to his life? (*Matthew 6.26–27*)

O LORD, you have searched me and you know me. You know when I sit and when I rise; you perceive my thoughts from afar. (*Psalm 139.1–2*)

As the rain and the snow come down from heaven, and do not return to it without watering the earth and making it bud and flourish, so that it yields seed for the sower and bread for the eater, so is my word that goes out from my mouth: It will not return to me empty, but will accomplish what I desire and achieve the purpose for which I sent it. (*Isaiah 55.10–11*)

The LORD is good, a refuge in times of trouble. He cares for those who trust in him. (*Nahum 1.7*)

continued >

lost in translation: the Bible

continued >

As you come to him, the living Stone – rejected by men but chosen by God and precious to him – you also, like living stones, are being built into a spiritual house to be a holy priesthood, offering spiritual sacrifices acceptable to God through Jesus Christ. (*1 Peter 2.4–5*)

He said, 'Go out and stand on the mountain before the LORD, for the LORD is about to pass by.' Now there was a great wind, so strong that it was splitting mountains and breaking rocks in pieces before the LORD, but the LORD was not in the wind; and after the wind an earthquake, but the LORD was not in the earthquake; and after the earthquake a fire, but the LORD was not in the fire; and after the fire a sound of sheer silence. (*1 Kings 19.11–12*)

Set me as a seal upon your heart, as a seal upon your arm; for love is strong as death, passion fierce as the grave. Its flashes are flashes of fire, a raging flame. Many waters cannot quench love, neither can floods drown it. If one offered for love all the wealth of one's house, it would be utterly scorned. (*Song of Solomon 8.6–7*)

Rend your heart and not your garments. Return to the LORD your God, for he is gracious and compassionate, slow to anger and abounding in love, and he relents from sending calamity. (*Joel 2.13*)

Come, let us return to the LORD; for it is he who has torn, and he will heal us; he has struck down, and he will bind us up. (*Hosea 6.1*)

He will wipe every tear from their eyes. Death will be no more; mourning and crying and pain will be no more, for the first things have passed away. (*Revelation 21.4*)

So I say to you: Ask and it will be given to you; seek and you will find; knock and the door will be opened to you. For everyone who asks receives; he who seeks finds; and to him who knocks, the door will be opened. (*Luke 11.9–10*)

He will judge between many peoples and will settle disputes for strong nations far and wide. They will beat their swords into ploughshares and their spears into pruning hooks. Nation will not take up sword against nation, nor will they train for war any more. (*Micah 4.3*)

I will take you from the nations, and gather you from all the countries, and bring you into your own land. I will sprinkle clean water upon you, and you shall be clean from all your uncleannesses, and from all your idols I will cleanse you. A new heart I will give you and a new spirit I will put within you; and I will remove from your body the heart of stone and give you a heart of flesh. (*Ezekiel 36.24–26*)

But Ruth replied, 'Don't urge me to leave you or to turn back from you. Where you go I will go, and where you stay I will stay. Your people will be my people and your God my God. Where you die I will die, and there I will be buried. May the Lord deal with me, be it ever so severely, if anything but death separates you and me.' (*Ruth 1.16–17*)

Dear friends, let us love one another, for love comes from God. Everyone who loves has been born of God and knows God. Whoever does not love does not know God, because God is love. (*1 John 4.7–8*)

lost in translation: the Bible

screen notes

The makeup of the Bible

Law/history

At the beginning of the Bible there are five books which as a group are called just that in Greek – 'the five books' or Pentateuch (meaning five books). The Jewish people call them the Torah or books of law. These books tell the early history of God's people (the people of Israel) including Moses receiving the laws for the people of Israel. Other books, such as Kings, tell the later history of the Jewish people. The Acts of the Apostles is a similar book about the early history of the Christian people or followers of the way.

Poetry/wisdom

Another five books in the Old Testament also fall in a group. They have a lot of word pictures or imagery. Some call these books poetic or wisdom literature. For example, you may know some of the Psalms. Some of them are now sung as hymns and worship songs.

Prophecy

Many of the books of the Old Testament contain visions which God sent to some people we call prophets. Not every word in these books is prophecy, some are about the lives of those prophets, like the story of Jonah. Some of the prophecies are also in very symbolic language so can take a little time to understand. Sometimes people also divide this group of books into the Major Prophets (the longer books) and the Minor Prophets (the shorter books towards the end of the Old Testament). The New Testament also finishes with a book of prophecy about the end of the world.

Gospels

The word 'gospel' means 'Good News'. The New Testament has four accounts of the Good News story of Jesus – those called Matthew, Mark, Luke and John. They are four different views of the life of Jesus. They have a lot in common and some contain bits which others don't. The author of the Gospel of Luke also wrote the Acts of the Apostles

Letters

Most of the New Testament is actually a collection of letters. Many of these were written by a man called Paul who never met Jesus during his lifetime but who saw him in a vision after Jesus had died and risen. Paul then travelled around to different cities preaching the Good News, then kept in touch via letter with the people he had preached to when he was elsewhere. They are a good source for people who have just started in faith as they are often written to people who have just heard about Jesus. There are also letters from Paul to individuals and letters from some of the disciples who are described in the Gospels and Acts.

lost in translation: the Bible

Bible bookcase

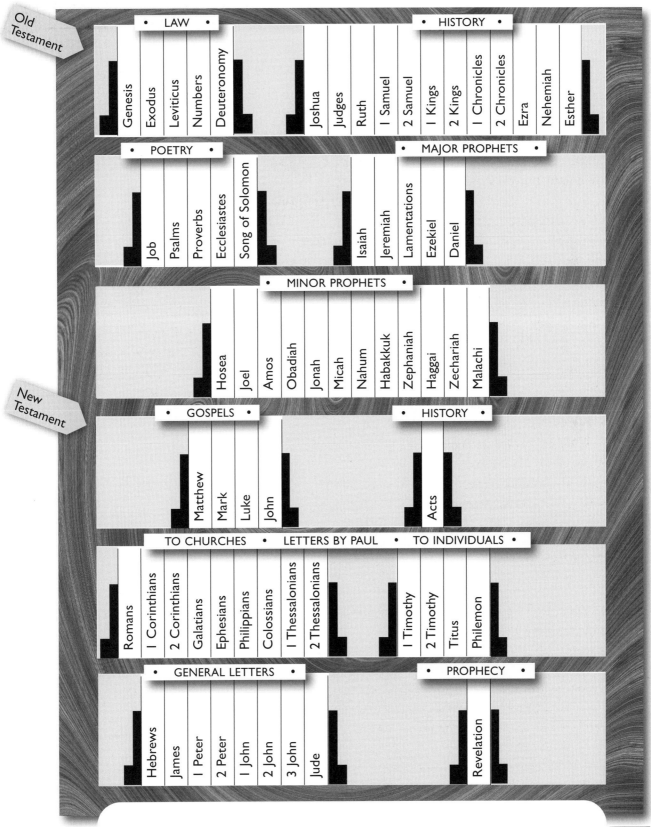

lost in translation: the Bible

screen notes

Books of the Bible

Genesis	Isaiah	Romans
Exodus	Jeremiah	1 Corinthians
Leviticus	Lamentations	2 Corinthians
Numbers	Ezekiel	Galatians
Deuteronomy	Daniel	Ephesians
Joshua	Hosea	Philippians
Judges	Joel	Colossians
Ruth	Amos	1 Thessalonians
1 Samuel	Obadiah	2 Thessalonians
2 Samuel	Jonah	1 Timothy
1 Kings	Micah	2 Timothy
2 Kings	Nahum	Titus
1 Chronicles	Habakkuk	Philemon
2 Chronicles	Zephaniah	Hebrews
Ezra	Haggai	James
Nehemiah	Zechariah	1 Peter
Esther	Malachi	2 Peter
Job	Matthew	1 John
Psalms	Mark	2 John
Proverbs	Luke	3 John
Ecclesiastes	John	Jude
Song of Solomon	Acts	Revelation

lost in translation: the Bible

Empty Bible bookcase

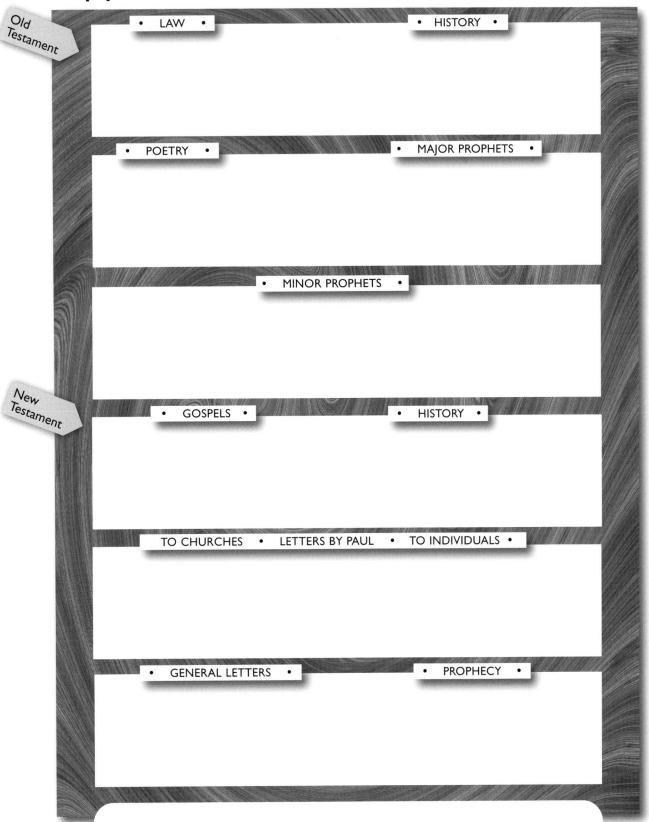

pay it forward: acts of the confirmed!

BILLBOARD

The aim of this session is to reflect on the group's experience of confirmation, to affirm their individual talents and consider if the group wants to continue meeting together

PLAN OF THE SESSION

The foyer	Discussion on how the confirmation service went	*(10 mins)*
Popcorn	Bible operation	*(5 mins)*
Trailers	A scene from *The Matrix* and discussion	*(10 mins)*
Action	Looking back at the film of our life	*(5 mins)*
Main feature	Gift boxes	*(20 mins)*
Credits	Prayer with gift boxes	*(10 mins)*
Review	Recap of what we have covered	*(5 mins)*
Forthcoming attractions	Discuss the future of the group	*(10 mins)*

Total running time: *75 mins*

Equipment list:
* 'Operation' game and passages on pieces of paper
* Storyboards from Session 1 if you still have them
* Small plain boxes or some nets for making small gift boxes
* Pieces of card
* Colouring pens
* Pencils
* Glue
* Scissors
* Tissue paper
* Sequins
* Stickers
* Other things to customize the boxes
* Music on CD
* DVD/video of *The Matrix*
* Bibles
* Flipchart and pens
* Refreshments

pay it forward: acts of the confirmed!

now showing

The aim of this session is to reflect on the group's experience of confirmation, to affirm their individual talents and consider if the group wants to continue meeting together.

popcorn

Use the game 'Operation' and replace the body parts with passages about the Church and get the young people to pick them out of the holes in turn. You could select passages they had chosen in the Bible session or passages relating to the Church as a body.

the foyer

This will be your first session after the confirmation service, and although you might have spoken to them on the day, you should let the group reflect as a whole:

- How did the day go?
- How did it feel?
- What did the Bishop say to you?
- What did other people say?

You might find it useful to pick up on the discussion in Session 5 when the group wrote down their expectations of the confirmation service.

- Did the confirmation service live up to these expectations?
- Did anything surprise them?

The group has now met for ten sessions covering the basics of Christian faith. Ask them:

- What have you enjoyed most?
- What did you find difficult?
- What would you like to know more about or discuss further?

Does the group want to continue to meet? If so, what sorts of things does the group want to do?

trailers

Introduce this week's theme: 'What next?'

In this section we will be looking at significant life events using a clip from *The Matrix*. For those who have not seen the film, Neo is a computer hacker who thinks there must be more to life, and a girl comes along and tells him he's right. The scene can be found at Chapter 7 20m 40s to 23m 00s.

> **'You have been down there, Neo. You know that road. You know exactly where it ends and I know that's not where you want to be.'**

Show the clip. Use these questions as a discussion starter:

- How do you think Neo felt during this scene?
- Do you feel you have stopped going down the same old path?
- Where do you think your path might be leading?
- Jesus doesn't hold a gun to our head but we've made a change. Does the change feel as dramatic?

pay it forward: acts of the confirmed!

action

If you have kept them, look back at the storyboards you made in Session 1. What would they now add? Think back to the Popcorn activity from the session on prayer. How would they show what happened at the confirmation if they were making a film about it?

Be sensitive to those who may not have had a really dramatic experience, but encourage them to share in the experience of others.

main feature

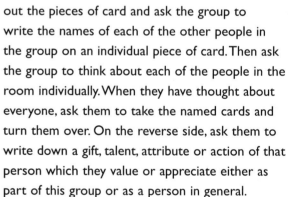

Find some small plain boxes or some nets for making small gift boxes and prepare some pieces of paper or card which will fit in the box. You will need one box for each member of the group (including leaders), and each person will need the same number of pieces of card to put in the boxes (i.e., if there are ten people in the group you will need ten boxes, and each of those ten people will need ten pieces of card, making 100 in all). Having some spare cards would also be a good idea. You will also need art materials to customize the boxes. If you have a local scrapstore (see Appendix 1) you could find a lot of these materials there. Be aware that this activity will take a little time to prepare. Set out the craft materials ready before the session

Give each member of the group a box for them to customize. Encourage them to be creative and make it represent them. During this time you can chat over how the course has been and what they might like to do as a group in the future.

When all the boxes are finished, place them together in a central place.

Pick some music to play in the background which won't distract the group from their task. Hand out the pieces of card and ask the group to write the names of each of the other people in the group on an individual piece of card. Then ask the group to think about each of the people in the room individually. When they have thought about everyone, ask them to take the named cards and turn them over. On the reverse side, ask them to write down a gift, talent, attribute or action of that person which they value or appreciate either as part of this group or as a person in general.

Allow them plenty of time for this, and be prepared to allow for some finishing sooner than others.

credits

When they have finished all of the cards, ask the group to place the cards in individual piles for each person with the name side of the card facing upwards. Then, as leaders, collect each pile and place the cards in the appropriate boxes still with the names facing upwards. Then hand them out to each member of the group.

Pray together a prayer of thanksgiving for our gifts and talents. You could use the prayer following.

continued >

pay it forward: acts of the confirmed!

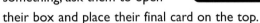

continued >

Lord, we thank you that you give each of us our own unique talents.

You have created a rich tapestry of humanity:

People who are kind and friendly to others.

Those who are wise and give good advice.

People who can run fast, jump high and excel in sports.

Talented musicians, artists, writers and builders.

For those who can teach and those who can listen.

Those who can love and those who can challenge.

Those who can explore and those who can build safe homes.

Lord, we thank you for these and all our gifts,

and for all the chances you give us to use them in service to you,

following the example of your Son, our Lord Jesus Christ. Amen.

Now play some more music and suggest that the group take the final card they have and think about their own talents. What talent would they like to develop? It could be a talent they already have, or a new one which they desire. They could write down a way in which they would like to use this talent. Make

credits

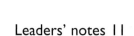

it clear that this is for them and does not need to be shared with the group if they don't want to. When everyone has written something, ask them to open their box and place their final card on the top.

Pray together for the development of the gifts of the group. You could use this prayer below.

Lord, we may have many gifts, or feel we have none.

We want to put our gifts to your service.

Lord, show us the people that you want us to be and the talents you want us to use.

Give us the faithfulness to grow these talents,

the patience to allow them to develop,

the wisdom to use them well,

the goodness to use them in the service of others,

the self-control to use them when needed without vanity,

the gentleness to work with others without agenda,

that we may find the joy and peace which comes from serving you.

So if we live by the Spirit, let us also be guided by the Spirit. Amen.

continued >

pay it forward: acts of the confirmed!

credits

continued >

Finally, play some more music and invite people to open their boxes. Tell them they can also wait until later when they are on their own if they want to.

If a discussion develops naturally, encourage it, but don't force people to share things if they don't want to.

extras

There are no Extras as we feel that this activity is suitable for all ages.

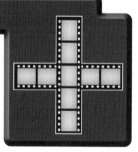

review

Each of us has our own individual talents, and God calls us to use them with love, joy, peace, patience, kindness, generosity, faithfulness, gentleness and self-control.

forthcoming attractions

If the group is going to continue to meet, agree a time and place, and if there is any preparation for them to do such as reading, give them the passages now.

deleted scenes

For younger groups you may prefer to use a clip from *Harry Potter* rather than *The Matrix*. Find the clip at Chapter 4 and play until 17m 11s in *Harry Potter and the Philosopher's Stone*. Hagrid is explaining that life is going to change very dramatically for Harry, and in ways that he could never imagine.

Alternatively, you could use the following clip from *Lemony Snicket's A Series of Unfortunate Events* where the children face a change in the future. This clip is at Chapter 1 02m 27s to 06m 18s.

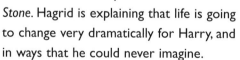

Additional games

Make your own movie

If you want to make the session a little longer at some point you could get the young people to make their own movie on a roll of paper to 'show' on their own miniature cinema (such as that at: <http://www.stane-island.net/pencilTV/pencilTV.htm>). Alternatively you could get young people to create a movie on Photo Story or Windows Movie Maker. Movie Maker uses film clips while Photo Story uses just pictures and words and will play them to music you select. The young people could make a movie of a Bible passage and then use it during the confirmation service.

Docufilm

How about getting a video camera and interviewing each of the young people about their expectations of the course, and later, perhaps after the confirmation service, asking them what it was like for them? You could then use this with new groups coming forward for confirmation.

A day in the life

For the section on church you could prepare in advance some interviews with people from the church, describing what they do. Or you could get young people to do that as part of their preparation for the session. You could also take photos of people and put them together into a poster, PowerPoint or Photo Story about the church for the group to look at.

Getaway

You might want to use some of these sessions as part of a weekend in preparation for the confirmation.

It might be good to do this with Sessions 6, 7, 8 and 9 or a selection of those. This way you could spend more time on the prayer activities and on looking at the Bible. You could also use some of the movie-making activities suggested, as well as show a whole movie in the evening such as *The Lion, the Witch and the Wardrobe, Star Wars: A New Hope,* or one of the others.

Session equipment lists

All sessions

Refreshments

Equipment, including sound, to play your DVDs

Session 1

DVD/video of *Bruce Almighty*

DVD/video of *Hitchhikers' Guide to the Galaxy*

Candle

Pens

Post-it notes

Flipchart and pens (or similar)

Storyboard handouts

CD player, appropriate music

Bibles

Session 2

DVD/video of *Big Fish*

Storyboard sheets

Bibles

Flipchart and pens

Postcards

Session 3

DVD/video of *Dogma*

Movie quiz question sheet

Pens

Slips of paper

Bibles

Copies of the Lord's Prayer

Session 4

Movie Magic grids prepared in advance

DVD/video of *Star Wars: A New Hope*

Jesus' words from the cross Screen Notes

A cockerel (a picture or a rubber chicken)*

Nails*

A hammer*

A ladder

Coins*

A sword

Wine*

A stick and sponge

A spear

A whip

A cloth*

Dice*

A cross (beams or a large piece of paper with a cross drawn on it)*

A crown of thorns*

*For each of these items you could substitute the item with a picture. We consider those marked * to be the most important.*

Session 5

DVD/video of *The Chronicles of Narnia – The Lion, the Witch and the Wardrobe*

Bibles

Flipchart and pens

Wallpaper (available from most scrapstores or cheap lining paper from a DIY shop)

Holy Spirit word cards

Session 6

DVD/video of *O Brother, Where Art Thou?*

Bibles

Flipchart and pens

Confirmation service sheet

Session 7

DVD/video of *The X-Men*

Bibles

Flipchart and pens

Film job sheets

Session 8

DVD/video of *Notting Hill*

Bibles

Flipchart and pens

Communion wafers

Session 9

DVD/video of *Meet the Parents*

Bibles

Flipchart and pens

Items relevant to the prayer modes you have selected, e.g. beads, icons, rosaries, etc.

Copies of Screen Notes

Session 10

DVD/video of *The Day After Tomorrow*

Bibles

Flipchart and pens

DVDs of different kinds

Images of Bible texts in Greek and Hebrew

Screen Notes

Session 11

'Operation' game and passages on pieces of paper

Storyboards from Session 1 if you still have them

Small plain boxes or some nets for making small gift boxes

Pieces of card

Colouring pens

Pencils

Glue

Scissors

Tissue paper

Sequins

Stickers

Other things to customize the boxes

Music on CD

DVD/video of *The Matrix*

Bibles

Flipchart and pens

Appendix 1: Useful websites/agencies

British Board of Film Classification

<http://www.bbfc.co.uk/>

As well as detailing the British classification of all films and the reason for the classification given in each case, this site gives links to sites for parents and students of film.

British Film Institute

<http://www.bfi.org.uk/education/>

The education section of the BFI has guidance on new films, especially those which are not the big blockbusters, as well as guidelines for those teaching and learning through film.

Canadian Menonite University's Movie Theology Section

<http://www.cmu.ca/library/faithfilm.html>

This offers a useful list of other sites and books about Christianity and film.

Christian Copyright Licensing International (CCLI)

<http://www.ccli.com/>

All you need to know about copyright licensing.

Christian Video Licensing International (CVLI)

<http://www.cvli.com/>

All you need to know about video licensing.

Church of England

<http://www.cofe.anglican.org/lifeevents/>

A section of the official website of the Church of England which explains the various life events celebrated by the church.

Christian Spotlight on Entertainment

<http://www.christiananswers.net/spotlight/>

A subsection of Christian Answers.net. This site is from the conservative evangelical outlook and includes morality ratings for films.

Christianity Today

<http://www.christianitytoday.com/biblestudies/movies/>

A site offering links to pay for download discussion guides for films.

Crosswalk

<http://www.crosswalk.com/movies/>

Reviews with useful cautions about the contents of films.

Damaris

<http://www.damaris.org/cw>

Under the Culture Watch section you will find films listed alphabetically with reviews and articles about particular aspects of the films and ways you can relate them to discussing the Christian faith.

Dark Matters

<http://darkmatt.blogspot.com/>

Regular reviews of current and forthcoming films by a funky Christian in Hitchin (one of the authors of *Reel Issues*) – just in case you can't keep up to date! Be warned that he rates films according to the following criteria:

> DARKMATTERS RATING SYSTEM (all ratings out of maximum 10 but '–' is bad whereas '+' is good): Endorphin Stimulation, Tasty Action, Gratuitous Babeness, Mind Blight/Boredom, Comedic Value and Arbitrary final rating.

The Daughters of St Paul

<http://www.daughtersofstpaul.com/mediastudies/reviews/index.html>

A Catholic outlook on films from the people who bring you Pauline books and media. The study guides are a little less user friendly but well worth a look.

The Evangelical Luteran Church in America

<http://www.elca.org/youth/reelworld/index.html>

A set of brief discussion guides for use after watching a whole film together.

The Faith and Film Circle (FFCC)

<http://www.faithandfilmcritics.com/>

This site is for Christians reviewing films and offers links to sites of its members. If you want a mature Christian reflection on a movie, this would be a perfect starting place.

Film Education

<http://www.filmeducation.org/resources.html>

This site is run by a charity sponsored by the British fiilm industry and is targeted at using films in RE lessons but is useful for age-differentiated use of films and seems to be updated regularly.

Hollywood Jesus

<http://www.hollywoodjesus.com/>

This site has been running since 1998 presenting reviews of films from a Christian perspective.

The Internet Movie Database

<http://www.imdb.com>

This is without question the best secular site for information about any film, giving all kinds of useful things including quotable bits and quirky facts.

Jesus Reel to Reel

<http://post.queensu.ca/~rsa/Real2Reel/realreel.htm>

This site originated as a resource for a graduate course called 'Jesus: Real to Reel' at the Institute of Pastoral Studies, Loyola University, Chicago. It includes a very comprehensive bibliography of books and articles on Christianity and film for those who want to take things a lot deeper.

Ministry and Media

<www.ministryandmedia.com>

This is a site from Group Publishing which you need to join to get at anything, but it is well worth it as it is regularly updated with themed video discussion starters and ways you can use current releases and DVDs with young people. You can search both by topic and by film for clips to use with groups, which makes this site very useful.

Movie Glimpse

<http://www.movieglimpse.com/>

A good site with thought-provoking reflections on films and links to Bible passages.

North East Religious Learning Resources Centre

<http://www.resourcescentreonline.co.uk/film-and-faith.html>

This site is designed for those wishing to use films in the context of religious education. It contains guidelines and a list of films with guidance and discussion points for each one.

Photo Story

<http://www.microsoft.com/windowsxp/using/digitalphotography/PhotoStory/default.mspx>

This is where you can download Photo Story 3 to help the young people make their own movies.

Reel Issues

<http://www.reelissues.org.uk/>

An excellent site from the Bible Society which offers some free material on individual films; to access all the good stuff you need to subscribe, but it looks worth it.

Refuel

<http://www.refuel.org.uk/curric/xphase/filmfaith/integrate.php>

A site from the Culham Institute aimed at those wanting to use film to enliven the RE curriculum at school. Some useful reflections on how different films can be used in different ways.

Scrapstores

<http://www.childrensscrapstore.co.uk/>

A site which describes what scrapstores are and includes a directory of scrapstores around the country.

Scripture Union – Connect Bible Studies

<http://www.scriptureunion.org.uk/>

If you search for 'Connect Bible Studies' you can find downloadable Bible studies linked to films (and other media). These can also be bought as books.

Textweek

<http://www.textweek.com/movies/themeindex.htm>

A good resource which is searchable by film and topic. It offers resources for each week of the lectionary and so also offers some searchability via Bible passage. It's not exhaustive or targeted directly at young people, so some of the content is oriented towards adult discussions.

WingClips

<http://www.wingclips.com/>

This modern and user-friendly page is an excellent site. It offers viewable and downloadable clips for schools and churches from new releases, as well as offering clip search by theme, film title, biblical references and film type (e.g. action, comedy).

Appendix 2: Filmography of films used in the book

Bernard and the Genie (PG)	Deleted scenes for Session 2
Big Fish (PG)	Session 2
Bruce Almighty (12)	Session 1
Charlie and the Chocolate Factory (PG)	Deleted scenes for Session 8
The Chronicles of Narnia –	
The Lion, the Witch and the Wardrobe (PG)	Session 5 and deleted scenes for Session 7
The Day After Tomorrow (12)	Session 10
Dogma (15)	Deleted scenes for Session 2
Evan Almighty (PG)	Session 1 and deleted scenes for Sessions 6 and 9
Gran Torino	Deleted scenes for Session 4
Harry Potter and the Order of the Phoenix (12)	Deleted scenes for Session 7
Harry Potter and the Philosopher's Stone (PG)	Deleted scenes for Session 11
Hitchhiker's Guide to the Galaxy (PG)	Session 1
Hook (U)	Deleted scenes for Session 8
The Incredibles (U)	Deleted scenes for Session 4
Jesus of Nazareth (PG)	Deleted scenes for Session 4
Lemony Snicket's A Series of Unfortunate Events (PG)	Deleted scenes for Session 11
The Life of Brian (15)	Deleted scenes for Session 2
The Man Who Sued God (15)	Deleted scenes for Session 1
The Matrix (15)	Session 11
Meet the Parents (PG)	Session 8
The Miracle Maker (U)	Deleted scenes for Sessions 2 and 4
Notting Hill (15)	Session 8
O Brother, Where Art Thou? (12)	Session 6
Pleasantville (12)	Deleted scenes for Session 1
Ratatouille (U)	Deleted scenes for Sessions 8, 9 and 10
Spiderman (12)	Deleted scenes for Session 6
Spirited Away (PG)	Deleted scenes for Session 7
Star Wars: A New Hope (U)	Session 4 and deleted scenes for Session 5
Talladega Nights: The Ballad of Ricky Bobby (12)	Deleted scenes for Session 8
The Passion of the Christ (18)	Deleted scenes for Session 4
The Seventh Seal (PG)	Deleted scenes for Session 8
Signs (12)	Deleted scenes for Session 8
The Truman Show (PG)	Deleted scenes for Session 1

Films by certification

U

Hook (U)	Deleted scenes for Session 8
The Incredibles (U)	Deleted scenes for Session 4
The Miracle Maker (U)	Deleted scenes for Session 2
Ratatouille (U)	Deleted scenes for Sessions 8, 9 and 10
Star Wars: A New Hope (U)	Session 4 and deleted scenes for Session 5

PG

Bernard and the Genie (PG)	Deleted scenes for Session 2
Big Fish (PG)	Session 2
Charlie and the Chocolate Factory (PG)	Deleted scenes for Session 8
The Chronicles of Narnia –	
The Lion, the Witch and the Wardrobe (PG)	Session 5 and deleted scenes for Session 7
Evan Almighty (PG)	Session 1 and deleted scenes for Sessions 6 and 9
Harry Potter and the Philosopher's Stone (PG)	Deleted scenes for Session 11
Hitchhiker's Guide to the Galaxy (PG)	Session 1
Jesus of Nazareth (PG)	Deleted scenes for Session 4
Lemony Snicket's A Series of Unfortunate Events (PG)	Deleted scenes for Session 11
Meet the Parents (PG)	Session 8
Spirited Away (PG)	Deleted scenes for Session 7
The Seventh Seal (PG)	Deleted scenes for Session 8
The Truman Show (PG)	Deleted scenes for Session 1

12

Bruce Almighty (12)	Session 1
The Day After Tomorrow (12)	Session 10
Harry Potter and the Order of the Phoenix (12)	Deleted scenes for Session 7
O Brother, Where Art Thou? (12)	Session 6
Pleasantville (12)	Deleted scenes for Session 1
Spiderman (12)	Deleted scenes for Session 6
Signs (12)	Deleted scenes for Session 8
Talladega Nights: The Ballad of Ricky Bobby (12)	Deleted scenes for Session 8

15

Dogma (15)	Deleted scenes for Session 2
Gran Torino (15)	Deleted scenes for Session 4
The Life of Brian (15)	Deleted scenes for Session 2
The Man Who Sued God (15)	Deleted scenes for Session 1
The Matrix (15)	Session 11
Notting Hill (15)	Session 8

18

The Passion of the Christ (18)	Deleted scenes for Session 4

Bibliography of books on faith and film

Mary Lea Bandy and Antonia Monda, eds, *Hidden God: Film and Faith* (Museum of Modern Art, 2003)

Catherine M. Barsotti and Robert K. Johnston, *Finding God in the Movies: 33 Films of Reel Faith* (Baker Books, 2004)

John Barton and John Muddiman, eds, *The Oxford Bible Commentary* (Oxford University Press, 2001)

Lloyd Baugh, *Imaging the Divine: Jesus and Christ-Figures in Film* (Sheed & Ward Ltd, 1997)

David S. Cunningham, *Reading Is Believing: The Christian Faith through Literature and Film* (Fleming H. Revell, 2002)

Christopher Deacy and Gaye Ortiz, *Theology and Film: Challenging the Sacred/Secular Divide* (Blackwell Publishing, 2007)

Christopher Deacy, *Faith in Film* (Ashgate, 2005)

Christopher Deacy, *Christianity and the Movies* (Ashgate, 2005)

Christopher Deacy, ed., *Screen Christologies: Redemption and the Medium of Film* (University of Wales Press, 2001)

Doug Fields and Eddie James, *Videos that Teach: Teachable Movie Moments from 75 Modern Film Classics* (Zondervan, 1999)

R. Douglas Geivett and James S. Spiegel, eds, *Faith, Film and Philosophy: Big Ideas on the Big Screen* (IVP Academic, 2007)

Gareth Higgins, *How Movies Helped Save My Soul: Finding Spiritual Fingerprints in Culturally Significant Films* (Relevant Books, 2003)

Robert Jewett, *St Paul Returns to the Movies: Triumph Over Shame* (Eerdmans, 1998)

Robert Jewett, *St Paul at the Movies* (Westminster, 1993)

Robert K. Johnston, *Reel Spirituality: Theology and Film in Dialogue* (Baker Books, 2000)

Richard Leonard, *Movies that Matter: Reading Film through the Lens of Faith* (Loyola University Press US, 2006)

Spencer Lewerenz and Barbara Nicolosi, eds, *Behind the Screen: Hollywood Insiders on Faith*, Film, *and Culture* (Baker Books, 2005)

J. C. Lyden, *Film as Religion: Myths, Morals, Rituals* (New York University Press, 2003)

Ian Maher, *Faith and Film: Close Encounters of an Evangelistic Kind* (Grove Books, 2002)

Ian Maher, *Reel Issues: Engaging Film and Faith* (The Bible Society, 1996)

P. Malone and R. Pacatte, *Lights, Camera, Faith* (Pauline Books and Media, 2001)

Clive Marsh, *Theology Goes to the Movies* (Routledge, 2007)

Clive Marsh, *Cinema and Sentiment: Film's Challenge to Theology* (Studies in Religion and Culture Series) (Paternoster Press, 2004)

Clive Marsh and Steve Moyise, *Jesus and the Gospels: An Introduction* (T & T Clark, 2005)

Clive Marsh and Gaye Ortiz, eds, *Explorations in Theology and Film: Movies and Meaning* (Blackwell, 1998)

Joel W. Martin and Conrad E. Ostwalt Jr, eds, *Screening the Sacred: Religion, Myth, and Ideology in Popular American Film* (Westview Press, 1995)

J. C. McDowell, *The Gospel According to 'Star Wars': Faith, Hope and the Force* (Westminster John Knox Press, 2007)

Edward McNulty, *Faith and Film: A Guidebook for Leaders* (Westminster/John Knox Press, 2007)

Edward McNulty, *Films and Faith: Forty Discussion Guides* (Viaticum Press, 1999) (includes discussion guides for the following films: *Amadeus*; *Babe*; *Babette's Feast*; *Boyz 'n the Hood*; *Broadway Danny Rose*; *A Bronx Tale*; *Chariots of Fire*; *Cool Hand Luke*; *Crimes and Misdemeanors*; *Cry Freedom*; *Dead Man Walking*; *Eleni*; *Field of Dreams*; *The Fisher King*; *Gandhi*; *The Gospel According to Matthew*; *Grand Canyon*; *The Great Santini*; *Hook*; *In the Name of the Father*; *The Joy Luck Club*; *The Long Walk Home*; *Matewan*; *The Mission*; *Network*; *On the Waterfront*; *Philadelphia*; *Places in the Heart*; *The Purple Rose of Cairo*; *The Pawn Broker*; *Romero*; *The Saint of Fort Washington*; *Schindler's List*; *Smoke*; *To Kill a Mockingbird*; *The Trip to Bountiful*; *Unforgiven*; *The War*; *The Wizard of Oz*; *The Year of Living Dangerously*)

Edward McNulty, *Praying the Movies* (Viaticum Press, 2001)

Margaret R. Miles, *Seeing and Believing: Religion and Values in the Movies* (Beacon Press, 1997)

Movie Clips for Kids: Faith-Building Video Devotions (Group Publishing, 2001)

Movie Clips for Kids – The Sequel (Group Publishing, 2004)

Mary Kay Mueller, Ben Forest and John Cantwell Kiley, *God Goes to Hollywood: A Movie Guide for the Modern Mystic* (iUniverse.com, 2000)

Connie Neal, *The Gospel According to Harry Potter: Spirituality in the Stories of the World's Favourite Seeker* (Westminster John Knox Press, 2002)

Gaye Ortiz, ed., *Explorations in Theology and Film: Movies and Meaning* (Blackwell, 1997)

Samuel J. Parvin, *Weekend at the Movies: The Best Retreats from Reel to Real* (Abingdon Press, 1999)

Mark I. Pinsky, *The Gospel According to Disney: Faith, Trust, and Pixie Dust* (Westminster John Knox Press, 2004)

J. Pungente SJ and M. Williams SJ, *Finding God in the Dark: Taking the Spiritual Exercises of St Ignatius to the Movies* (Novalis, 2004)

Reel to Real: Making the Most of the Movies with Youth (Abingdon Press, 1999)

Theresa Sanders, *Celluloid Saints: Images of Sanctity in Film* (Mercer University Press, 2002)

Tim Sledge and Ally Barrett, *Get a Life!: A Five-session Course on Life Goals for Young People* (Church House Publishing, 2008)

Richard C. Stern, *Savior on the Silver Screen* (Paulist Press International, 1999)

Mark Stibbe and J. John, *Passion for the Movies: Spiritual Insights from Contemporary Films* (Authentic Lifestyle, 2005)

Mark Stibbe and J. John, *The Big Picture 2: More Spiritual Insights from Modern Movies* (Authentic Lifestyle, 2003)

Mark Stibbe and J. John, *The Big Picture: Finding the Spiritual Message in Movies: v. I* (Authentic Lifestyle, 2002)

Bryan P. Stone, *Faith and Film: Theological Themes at the Cinema* (Chalice Press, 2000)

W. Barnes Tatum, *Jesus at the Movies* (Polebridge Press, 2000)

William Telford, Eric S. Christianson and Peter Francis, eds, *Cinema Divinite: Religion, Theology and the Bible in Film* (SCM Press, 2005)

Sara Anson Vauz, *Finding Meaning at the Movies* (Abingdon Press, 1999)

Richard Walsh, *Reading the Gospels in the Dark: Portrayals of Jesus in Film* (The Athlone Press, 2003)

David Wenham and Steve Walton, *Exploring the New Testament: Introducing the Gospels and Acts* (SPCK, 2001)

Ralph Wood, *The Gospel According to Tolkien: Visions of the Kingdom in Middle-Earth* (Westminster John Knox Press, 2003)

Melanie J, Wright, *Religion and Film: An Introduction* (I B Tauris & Co Ltd, 2006)

Mark Yaconelli, *Contemplative Youth Ministry* (SPCK, 2006)